contemporary R&B

PIANO・VOCAL・GUITAR

ISBN 0-634-01714-4

HAL·LEONARD®
CORPORATION
7777 W. BLUEMOUND RD. P.O. BOX 13819 MILWAUKEE, WI 53213

For all works contained herein:
Unauthorized copying, arranging, adapting, recording or public performance is an infringement of copyright.
Infringers are liable under the law.

Visit Hal Leonard Online at
www.halleonard.com

Song list and artists

- All My Life 4
  H-Ci & JoJo
- Bills, Bills, Bills 13
  Destiny's Child
- The Boy Is Mine 20
  Brandy & Monica
- Bring It All to Me 27
  Blaque
- Bug A Boo 34
  Destiny's Child
- Chanté's Got a Man 42
  Chanté Moore
- Count On Me 48
  Whitney Houston & CeCe Winans
- Don't Take It Personal (Just One of Dem Days) 54
  Monica
- Doo Wop (That Thing) 64
  Lauryn Hill
- Exhale (Shoop Shoop) 61
  Whitney Houston
- The First Night 70
  Monica
- 4 Seasons of Loneliness 76
  Boyz II Men
- Get It On Tonite 82
  Montell Jordan
- Gettin' Jiggy Wit It 90
  Will Smith
- Heartbreak Hotel 92
  Whitney Houston
- Heartbreaker 99
  Mariah Carey featuring Jay-Z
- I Get Lonely 106
  Janet
- I'll Be Missing You 112
  Puff Daddy & Faith Evans (featuring 112)
- It's Not Right but It's Okay 118
  Whitney Houston
- It's So Hard to Say Goodbye to Yesterday 127
  Boyz II Men
- My Way 130
  Usher
- Nice & Slow 136
  Usher
- No Matter What 142
  Boyzone
- No Scrubs 152
  TLC
- Nobody 158
  Keith Sweat featuring Athena Cage
- On and On 147
  Erykah Badu
- Satisfy You 162
  Puff Daddy featuring R. Kelly
- Sittin' Up in My Room 167
  Brandy
- Tell Me It's Real 172
  H-Ci & JoJo
- Together Again 182
  Janet
- Unpretty 189
  TLC
- When You Believe (from THE PRINCE OF EGYPT) 196
  Whitney Houston and Mariah Carey
- Wild Wild West 210
  Will Smith featuring Dru Hill & Kool Moe Dee
- You Make Me Wanna... 203
  Usher
- You're Makin' Me High 218
  Toni Braxton

ALL MY LIFE

Words by JOEL HAILEY
Music by JOEL HAILEY and RORY BENNETT

Slowly, somewhat freely

With pedal

Ba-by, ba-by, ba-by, ba-by, ba-by, ba-by,

Slowly, steadily

ba-by, ba-by, ba-by, ba-by, babe.
(Vocal 1st time only)

Original key: D♭ major. This edition has been transposed down one half-step to be more playable.

© 1997 EMI APRIL MUSIC INC., CORD KAYLA MUSIC and HEE BEE DOOINIT MUSIC
All Rights for CORD KAYLA MUSIC Controlled and Administered by EMI APRIL MUSIC INC.
All Rights Reserved   International Copyright Secured   Used by Permission

I will never find another lover sweeter than you, sweeter than you. And I will never find another

lov-er more pre-cious than you, ____ more pre-cious than you. ___ Girl, you are close to me, you're like my moth-er, close to me, you're like my fa-ther, close to me, you're like my sis-ter, close to me, you're like my broth-er. You are the on - ly one. ___ You're my ev-'ry-thing and for you ___ this song ___ I sing. ___ all my life ___
And

I prayed for some-one like you and I thank God that I, that I fin-al-ly found you. For all my life I prayed for some-one like you, and I hope that you

G Am G/B C G/B Am
feel the same way too. Yes, I
To Coda
F G Am G Am G/B C
pray that you do love me too. I said you're
Am7 F Gsus
3 fr
all that I'm think - ing of.
C Am7 F
Da, da, da, da, da. Da, da, da, da, da. Da, da, da, da, da. Da, da,

Gsus
3 fr
C
C/B
Am
da, da, da. Said I prom-ise to nev-er fall in love ___ with a strang - er.
F(add2)
Gsus
3 fr
Am7
You're all I'm think-ing of. I praise the Lord a - bove for send-ing me your love.
Fmaj7
Dm9
G
D.S. al Coda
I cher-ish ev-'ry hug. I real-ly love you.
For
CODA
G
Am
G/B
Dm
do love ___ me. You're all ___ that ___ I ev -

-er know. When you smile on my face, all I see is a glow. You turned my life a-round. You picked me up when I was down. You're all that I ev-er know. When you smile life is glow. You picked me up when I was down. Say'n you're all that I ev-er know.

When you smile life is glow. You picked me up when I was down. And I hope that you feel the same way too. Yes, I pray that you do love me too. In all my life

I prayed for some-one like you and I thank God that I, that I fin-al-ly found you. For all my life I prayed for some-one like you. Yes, I you.

BILLS, BILLS, BILLS

Words and Music by KANDI L. BURRUSS,
KEVIN BRIGGS, BEYONCÉ KNOWLES,
KELLY ROWLAND and LE TOYA LUCKETT

Moderately, half-time feel

At first we start-ed out real cool, tak-in' me pla-ces I had nev-er been. But now
Now you've been max-in' out my card, gave me bad cred-it, buy me gifts with my own name.

© 1999 EMI APRIL MUSIC INC., AIR CONTROL MUSIC, KANDACY MUSIC, HITCO MUSIC, SHEK'EM DOWN MUSIC,
BEYONCE PUBLISHING, KELENDRIA MUSIC PUBLISHING and LETOYA MUSIC PUBLISHING
All Rights for AIR CONTROL MUSIC and KANDACY MUSIC Controlled and Administered by EMI APRIL MUSIC INC.
All Rights Reserved   International Copyright Secured   Used by Permission

14

Em7 | **F#**

_____ you're get-ting comf'-ta-ble, ain't do-in' those things you did no more. You're
_____ Have-n't paid the first bill, but you're stead-y head-in' to the mall, goin' on

Em7 | **F#**

slow-ly mak-in' me pay for things your mon-ey should be han-dl-ing. _____
shop-pin' sprees _____ per-pe-trat-in' to your friends that you be ball-in'. _____

Bm | **F#** **Bm**

And now you ask to use my car. Drive it all day and don't fill
And then you use my cell-phone, call-in' who-ev-er that you

F# | **Em7**

up the _____ tank. _____ And you _____ have the au-dac-i-ty to
think at _____ home. _____ And then _____ when the bill comes, all of a

15

16

[F#] need some-one to help me out, in-stead of a scrub like you [Em7]

[F#] who don't know what a man's a-bout. Can you pay my bills? Can you [Bm]

[A#dim] pay my tel-e-phone bills? Do you pay my au-to-mo-bills? If you [A]

[E/G#] did then may-be we could chill. I don't think you do, so [N.C.] [G]

17

18

Bm   **A#dim**

You tri - fl - in' good - for - noth - in' type of broth - er.

Bm   **A#dim**   **Play 4 times**

Oh, sil - ly me, why have - n't I found an - oth - er?

Bm   **A#dim**

Can you pay my bills? Can you pay my tel - e - phone bills? Do you
Lead vocal ad lib

A   **E/G#**

pay my au - to - mo - bills? If you did than may - be we could chill.

N.C.
G
F♯
N.C.
Play 3 times
I don't think you do, so you and me are through.
N.C.
Can you pay my bills? Can you pay my tel - e - phone bills? Do you
pay my au - to - mo - bills? If you did then may - be we could chill.
I don't think you do, so you and me are through.

THE BOY IS MINE

Words and Music by LaSHAWN DANIELS,
JAPHE TEJEDA, RODNEY JERKINS,
FRED JERKINS and BRANDY NORWOOD

Brandy: Excuse me, can I please talk to you for a minute? *Monica:* Uh huh, sure. You know, you look kind of familiar. *Brandy:* Yeah, you do too. But, um, I just wanted to know, do you know

© 1998 EMI APRIL MUSIC INC., LaSHAWN DANIELS PRODUCTIONS, HENCHI MUSIC, EMI BLACKWOOD MUSIC INC.,
RODNEY JERKINS PRODUCTIONS, FRED JERKINS PUBLISHING, ENSIGN MUSIC CORPORATION and BRAN-BRAN MUSIC
All Rights for LaSHAWN DANIELS PRODUCTIONS and HENCHI MUSIC Controlled and Administered by EMI APRIL MUSIC INC.
All Rights for RODNEY JERKINS PRODUCTIONS Controlled and Administered by EMI BLACKWOOD MUSIC INC.
All Rights Reserved   International Copyright Secured   Used by Permission

somebody named... You know his name. Monica: Oh, yeah, definitely. I know his name.

Brandy: Well, I just want to let you know that he's mine. Monica: Heh, no no. He's mine.

You need to give it up; I've had about enough. It's not hard to see; the boy is mine. I'm sorry that you seem to be con-

22

C♯m9
but you're blind if you can't see that his love is all in me.
he is a part of my life. I know it's kill - ing you in - side.
F♯m9
2 fr
See, I tried to hes - i - tate; I did - n't want to say what he told me,
You can say what you wan - na say, what we have you can't take.
C♯m9
he said with - out me he could - n't make it through the day. Ain't that a shame?
From the truth you can't es - cape. I can tell the re - al from the fake.
F♯m9
2 fr
But may - be you mis - un - der - stood 'cause I can't see how he could
When will you get the pic - ture? You're the past and I'm fu - ture.

want to tell you some-thing that's so good, for my love is all it took.
Get a-way, it's my time to shine. If you didn't know, the boy is mine.
The boy is mine. You need to give it up;

D.S. al Coda

CODA
mine. You need to give it up; I've had a-bout e-nough. It's not hard to see; the boy is mine. I'm sor-ry that you seem to be con-fused. He be-longs to

1
F#m9
2fr
2
F#m9
2fr
me; the boy is mine._ You need to give it __ mine._ I can be sure it's love_ I've found,_
C#m9
___ you sim - ply can't, I won't _ al - low. ___ The boy __ is mine with - out __ a doubt._
F#m9
2fr
___ You might _ as well throw in ___ the towel. ______ What makes you think that he __ wants you _
C#m9
___ when I'm the one that brought _ him to ___ the spe - cial place that's in ___ my heart?_

He was my lov-er from the start.
The boy is mine. You need to give it up; I've had a-bout e-nough. It's not hard to see; the boy is mine. I'm sor-ry that you seem to be con-fused. He be-longs to me; the boy is mine. You need to give it me. The boy is mine.

BRING IT ALL TO ME

Words and Music by KEVIN SPENCER, WILLIAM SHELBY,
NIDRA BEARD, LINDA CARRIERE, CORY ROONEY,
B. LAWRENCE, V. RUBY and L. LEWIS

Moderately, not too fast

* *Male vocal written one octave lower than sung throughout.*

fine as can be ____ in your fan-cy car. ____
for-ward if I ____ told you how I feel? ____

I can tell you're look-in' at me. ____ What-'cha wan-na do? ____
That's just the way I do my thing. ____ I'm so for real. ____

Are you just gon-na sit there and stare? ____
Are you feel-in' my Timb's, my bag-gy jeans,

Ba - by, talk to me. ____
my thug ap - peal?

Gm7
3 fr
D
Tell me what's on your mind,
Do you like it when a man can keep it
Gm7
3 fr
F
Gm7
3 fr
ba - by, oh.
real, oh?
(Female:) Oh, ba - by, bring it all to me.
C
Gm7
3 fr
F
Bring it on. But I don't need no fan - cy
Gm7
3 fr
D
cars or dia - mond rings. Ba - by, I don't need, no.

30

I'll put my pride to the side just to tell you how good you make me feel inside.

(Male:) There's not a single question that we can't make this right 'cause it's you I need

ev - 'ry day ____ and *(Both:)* night, ____ oh.

(Female:) Oh, ba - by, bring it all to me. ____
Lead vocal ad lib.

But I don't need no fan - cy cars and dia - mond rings. ____

Oh, ba - by,

bring it all to me. _____ Gim - me your

time, your love, your space, your en - er - gy. _____

Repeat and Fade

Optional Ending

BUG A BOO

Words and Music by KANDI L. BURRUSS,
KEVIN BRIGGS, BEYONCÉ KNOWLES, KELLY ROWLAND,
LE TOYA LUCKETT and LATAVIA ROBERSON

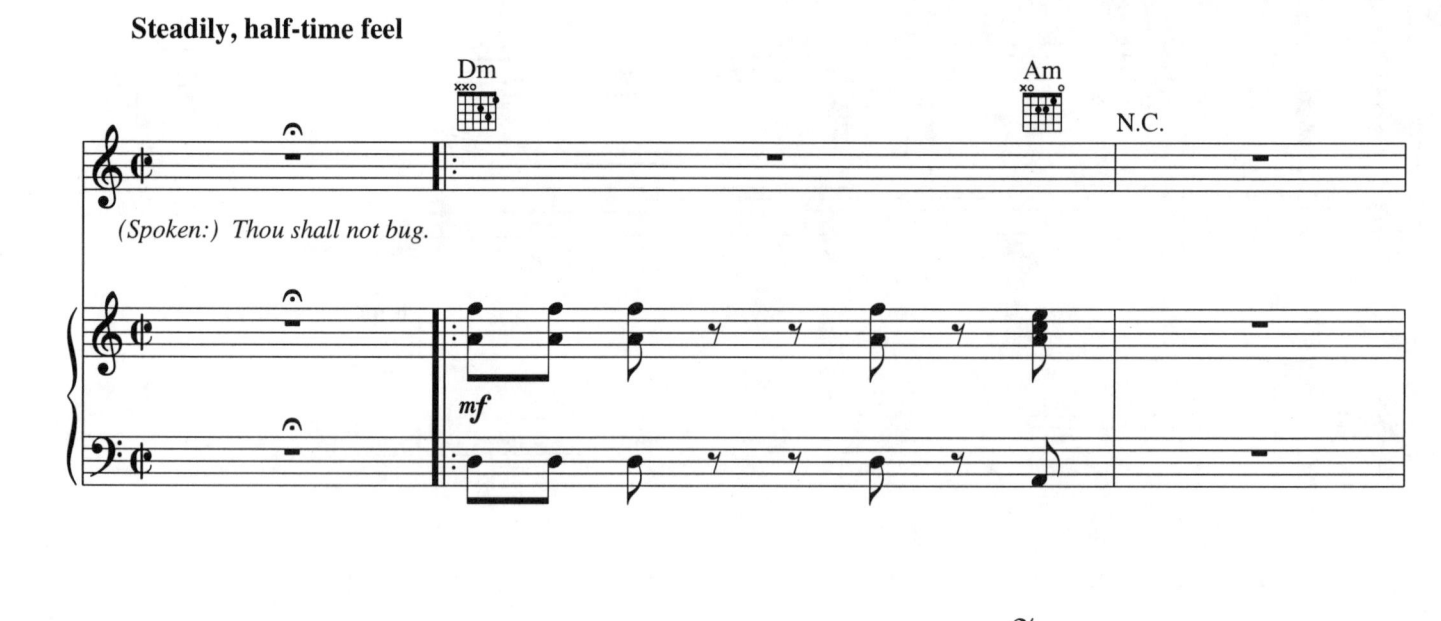

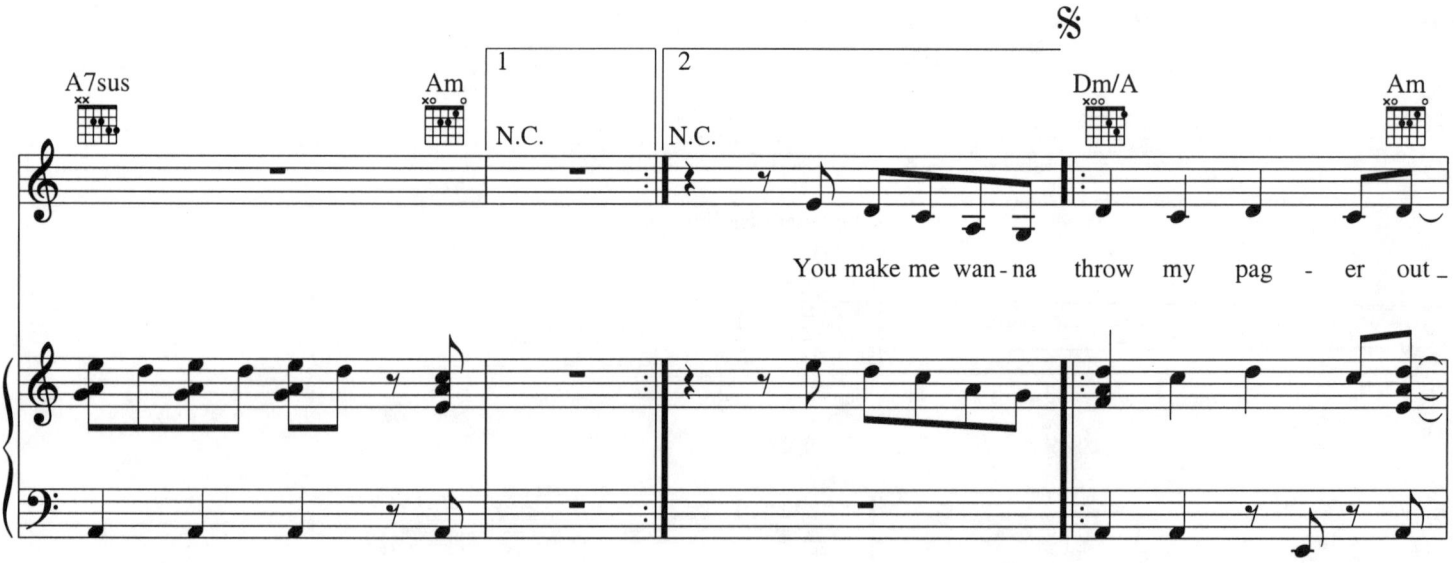

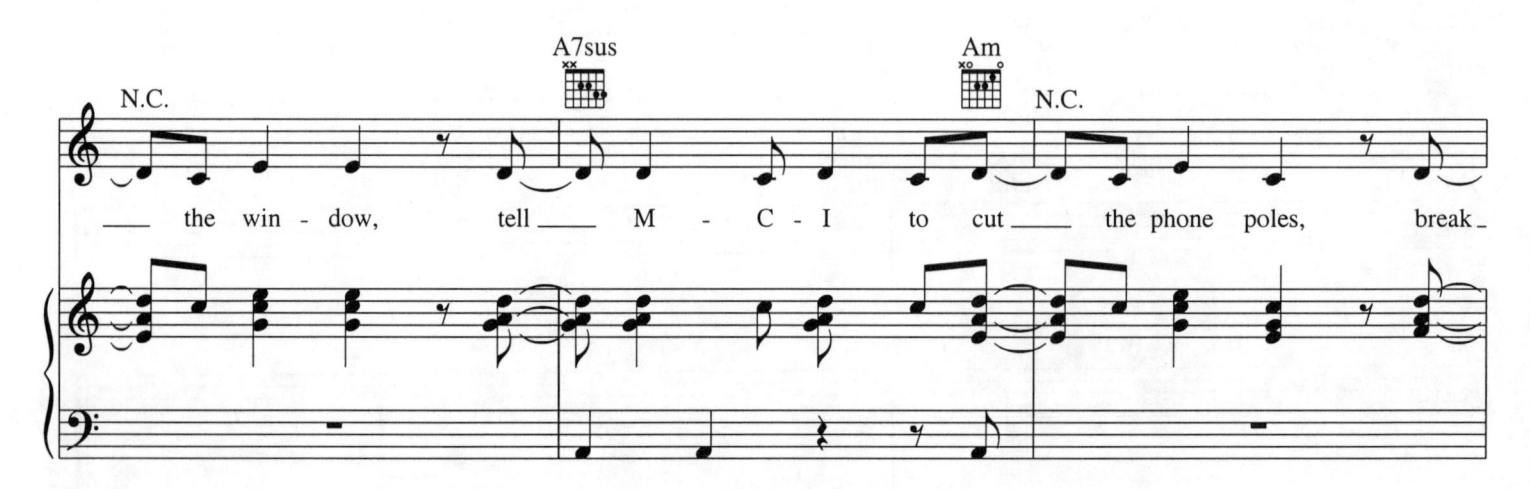

Steadily, half-time feel

(Spoken:) Thou shall not bug.

You make me wan-na throw my pag-er out the win-dow, tell M-C-I to cut the phone poles, break

Original key: A♭ minor. This edition has been transposed up one half-step to be more playable.

© 1999 EMI APRIL MUSIC INC., AIR CONTROL MUSIC, KANDACY MUSIC, HITCO MUSIC, SHEK'EM DOWN MUSIC,
BEYONCE PUBLISHING, KELENDRIA MUSIC PUBLISHING, LETOYA MUSIC PUBLISHING and LATAVIA MUSIC PUBLISHING
All Rights for AIR CONTROL MUSIC and KANDACY MUSIC Controlled and Administered by EMI APRIL MUSIC INC.
All Rights for HITCO MUSIC Administered by WINDSWEPT PACIFIC SONGS
All Rights Reserved   International Copyright Secured   Used by Permission

Dm/A Am N.C. A7sus Am
my lease so I can move 'cause you a bug a boo, a bug a
N.C. Dm/A Am N.C.
boo. I wan-na put your num-ber on the call block, have
A7sus Am N.C. Dm/A Am
A-O-L make my e-mail stop 'cause you a bug a boo. You're bug-gin'
To Coda
N.C. A7sus Am N.C.
what, you're bug-gin' who, you're bug-gin' me and don't you see it ain't cool. It's

not hot { that you be callin' me, stressin' me, pagin' my beeper. You're just non-
when I'm blockin' your phone number you call me over your best friends

stop. And it's not hot that you be leavin' me messages ev'ry
house. And it's not hot that I can't even go out with my girlfriends

ten minutes and then you stop by. When I first met you you were cool,
without you trackin' me down. You need to chill out with that miss

but it was game. You had me fooled 'cause twenty min-
'cause you can't keep havin' me stressed 'cause ev'ry time

-utes af-ter I ___ gave you my num-ber you al-read-y had my mail-box
___ my phone _ rings it ___ seems to be you and I'm pray-in' that it is some-one
full. _____
else. _____ So what? You bought a pair of shoes. What? Now, I
guess you think I owe you. You don't have to call as much as you
do. I'd give 'em back to be through wit' you. ___ And so

what? My mom-ma likes you. What? Now, I guess you think I will, too. E-ven if the Pope said he liked you too, I don't real-ly care 'cause you're a bug a boo. You make me wan-na I don't give a damn 'cause you're a bug a boo. You make me wan-na

D.S. al Coda

CODA

cool. When you call me on the phone, you're bug-gin' me. When you fol-low me a-round, you're bug-gin' me. Ev-'ry-thing you do be bug-gin' me. You're bug-gin' me. You're bug-gin' me. When you show up at my door, you're bug-gin' me. When you o-pen up your mouth, you're bug - gin' me. Ev - 'ry time I see your face, you're bug - gin' me. You're bug - gin' me. You're bug - gin' me. You make me wan - na throw my pag - er out the win - dow, tell M-C-I to cut the phone poles, break my lease so I can move 'cause you a bug a boo, a bug a

(Lead vocal-ad lib.)

41

CHANTÉ'S GOT A MAN

Words and Music by GEORGE FRANKLIN JACKSON,
JAMES HARRIS III, TERRY LEWIS,
CHANTÉ MOORE and JAMES WRIGHT

In a slow two

Chan-té's got a man at home. And he's so good to me. I'm sor-ry that your man ain't home.
Now why'd you let him beat you down?

I'm sor-ry that he all left you a-lone.
What's up with that? There's good men a-round.

© 1999 SCREEN GEMS-EMI MUSIC INC., EMI APRIL MUSIC INC., FLYTE TYME TUNES INC.,
MINNEAPOLIS GUYS MUSIC, JI BRANDA MUSIC WORKS, EMI BLACKWOOD MUSIC INC. and CHANTÉ 7 PUBLISHING
All Rights for FLYTE TYME TUNES INC., MINNEAPOLIS GUYS MUSIC and JI BRANDA MUSIC WORKS Controlled and Administered by EMI APRIL MUSIC INC.
All Rights for CHANTÉ 7 PUBLISHING Controlled and Administered by EMI BLACKWOOD MUSIC INC.
All Rights Reserved   International Copyright Secured   Used by Permission
- contains a sample of "One Bad Apple Don't Spoil The Whole Bunch"

G#7#5(#9)
4fr
C#m7
4fr
A6/9
G#7#5(♭9)
4fr
Mm.
It's such a shame ___ your man is play-ing games.
Don't you know how beau-ti-ful you are in-side, ______ girl.
6
C#m7
4fr
A6/9
I heard you say ________ that men are
And don't you let no - bod - y go and steal your pride._
F#m7
G#m7
4fr
A
all the same. ______________ No no no.
______________________ No no no.
It's not the truth, girl._ 'Cause I got
B
B#dim7
proof, girl._ I got a man at home. ______________________

44

2
G♯7 G♯7/B♯ A(add2) B
I once was where you are. Thought men were all the same.
he's so good to me.
B♯dim7
N.C.
But I nev - er gave up hope and now my life has changed.
N.C.
Em Bm7 C Bm Em11 G/B
Lis - ten to me, girl. One bad ap - ple don't spoil the
Am G F♯7♯5(♭9) C7/B♭ B7♯5(♯9) Em7 A7
whole bunch, girl. He al - ways treats me right. We nev - er fight. He

sends me flow-ers. He wines and dines me. Took me home to meet his ma-ma. How he loves me. One bad ap-ple don't spoil the whole bunch, girl. Oh, if you give it one more try be-fore you give up on love. *(Spoken:)* That's my man calling me.

C♯m7 G♯m7 Amaj9 C♯m7 F♯m7 G♯7♯5 C♯m7 G♯m7
Chan-té's got a man at home. It hurts me your man's
Amaj9 C♯m7 F♯m7 G♯7♯5(♯9) C♯m7 G♯m7
leav-ing you all a - lone. I can't help it that your
Amaj9 C♯m7 F♯m7 G♯m7
Repeat and Fade
ba - by's been creep-in' at and cheat-in' on you, beat - ing on you.
Optional Ending
C♯m7 G♯m7 Amaj9 C♯m7 F♯m7 G♯7 G♯7/B♯ C♯m7
Chan-té's got a man at home.

COUNT ON ME
from WAITING TO EXHALE

Words and Music by BABYFACE,
WHITNEY HOUSTON and MICHAEL HOUSTON

Slowly ♩ = 56

Chorus:

Count on me _ through thick _ and thin, a friend- ship that _ will nev- er end. When you _ are weak, _ I will _ be strong, _ help- ing you _ to car- ry on. _ Call on me, _ I will _ be there. _

Copyright © 1995 Sony/ATV Songs LLC, ECAF Music, Fox Film Music Corp., Nippy Music and Aurianna Publishing
All Rights on behalf of Sony/ATV Songs LLC and ECAF Music Administered by Sony/ATV Music Publishing, 8 Music Square West, Nashville, TN 37203
International Copyright Secured   All Rights Reserved

Em7 F# Bm Em11 7fr D/F#
Don't be a - fraid. Please be - lieve _ me when _ I say, _
Em9/A Dmaj7 Em7
count on. _ I can see _ it's hurt - ing you. _
Dmaj7/F# Em7 Dmaj7 Em7
I can feel _ your pain. _ It's hard to see _ the sun - shine through _ the
Am9 5fr D7 Gmaj9 A7/G
rain. _ I know some-times _ it seems _ as if it's

F♯m7
Bm7
2fr
Em7
nev - er gon - na end, _ but you'll get through it, just
Em9/A
Chorus:
D
Em7
don't _ give in. 'Cause you can count on me _ through thick _ and thin, a friend -
D/F♯
Gmaj13
3fr
D/A
A/G
- ship that _ will nev - er end. When you _ are weak, _ I will _ be strong, _
D(9)/F♯
G(9)
Dmaj7/F♯
Bm
help - ing you _ to car - ry on. _ Call on me, _ I will _ be there. _

Em7 F♯ Bm Em11 D/F♯
To Coda I
To Coda II
7fr
Don't be a - fraid. Please be - lieve me when I say,
Em7/A D Em7
count on, you can count on me. Ah,
D/F♯ Em7 D Em7 Am7 D7
yes you can. I know
Bridge:
Gmaj9 A/G F♯m7 Bm
some - times it seems as if we're stand-in' all a - lone. But

we'll get through it, 'cause love won't let __ us fold. __

Coda I

count on. __ There's a place in-side _ of all _ of us where our faith in love _ be-gins. _ You should reach _ to find _ the truth _ in love, the an-swer's there _ with-in. _ I know _ that life _ can make _ you feel it's much

F♯m7
Bm
Em7
Em7/A
D.S. 𝄋 al Coda II
hard-er than _ it real-ly is, __ but we'll get through it, just don't, don't give _ in.
Coda II
F♯m/A Em7/A
count on, count on, count on, count on, count on, count on, count on
Dmaj7
Em7
Dmaj7
Em7
me. __ Ah, yes you can, _
Dmaj7
Em7
Dmaj7
know I can, oh yeah. _ count on me. __
__ sure you can, So glad I can _ count on me, __

DON'T TAKE IT PERSONAL
(Just One of Dem Days)

Words and Music by DALLAS AUSTIN, DEREK SIMMONS,
QUINCY D. JONES III and LL COOL J

Moderately

It's just one of dem days when I wan-na be all a-lone. It's just one of dem days when I got-ta be all a-lone. It's just one of dem days, don't take it per-son-al. I just wan-na be all a-lone when you think I treat you wrong.

© 1995 EMI APRIL MUSIC INC., DARP MUSIC, AFRO DREDITE MUSIC, WINDSWEPT PACIFIC ENTERTAINMENT CO. d/b/a FULL KEEL MUSIC CO.,
DEEP TECHNOLOGY MUSIC, DEF JAM MUSIC, INC., LL COOL J MUSIC and NU RHYTHM AND LIFE MUSIC
All Rights for DARP MUSIC Controlled and Administered by EMI APRIL MUSIC INC.
All Rights for DEEP TECHNOLOGY MUSIC Administered by WINDSWEPT PACIFIC ENTERTAINMENT CO. d/b/a FULL KEEL MUSIC CO.
All Rights Reserved   International Copyright Secured   Used by Permission

E♭
3 fr
I wan-na take some time out _ to _ think things through. I know it
Cm
3 fr
al - ways feels like I'm do-in' you wrong,_ but I'm so in love _ with you. So,
E♭
3 fr
un - der-stand _ that I'm on - ly in love. You're the on - ly one _ I need. _ So, have
_ no thought_ that I want _ to leave,_ and ba - by, trust _ me, please. _ Just one of dem

56

Cm7

days that a girl goes through. When I'm an-gry in-side, don't wan-na take it

Eb

out on you. Just one of dem things don't take it per-son-al. I just

Cm7   N.C.   Eb

wan-na be all a-lone when you think I treat you wrong. Don't take it per-son-al.

Ba-by, ba-by, ba-by, ba-by, ba-by.
Don't take it per-son-al.

57

there for you when you need me, boy. So, baby, don't you leave. Just one of dem days that a girl goes through. When I'm angry inside, don't wanna take it out on you. Just one of dem things, don't take it personal. I just wanna be all alone when you think I treat you wrong. *Solo ends* Just one of dem days that a girl goes through. When I'm angry in-side, I don't wanna take it out on you. Just one of dem things, don't take it per-son-al. I just wan-na be all a-lone when you think I treat you wrong. Don't take it

per - son - al. _____ Ba - by, ba - by, ba - by, ba - by, ba - by. Don't take it

per - son - al. _____

D.S. al Coda

CODA

per - son - al, __ ba - by, per - son - al, __ ba - by. __

Repeat and Fade

Per - son - al, __ ba - by, per - son - al, __ ba - by; __

EXHALE (SHOOP SHOOP)
from the Original Soundtrack Album WAITING TO EXHALE

Words and Music by
BABYFACE

Easy R&B ballad

1. Ev-'ry-one falls in love some-times. Some-times it's wrong
2.,3. laugh, some-times you'll cry. Life nev-er tells us

and some-times it's right. For ev-'ry
the whens or whys. When you've got

win some-one must fail, but there comes a
friends to wish you well, you'll find a

Copyright © 1995 Sony/ATV Songs LLC, ECAF Music and Fox Film Corporation
All Rights on behalf of Sony/ATV Songs LLC and ECAF Music Administered by Sony/ATV Music Publishing, 8 Music Square West, Nashville, TN 37203
International Copyright Secured All Rights Reserved

Dm7
C
point when, when we ex - hale, yeah, yeah.
point when you will ex - hale, yeah, yeah.
Say,
F(add9)
C/E
Dm7
shoop shoop shoop shoo be doo. Shoop shoop shoo be doo. Shoop shoop shoo be
C
F(add9)
doo. Shoop shoop shoo be doo. Shoop shoop shoo be
C/E
Dm7
1
C
To Coda
doo. Shoop shoop shoo be doo. Shoop shoop shoo be doo. Some-times you'll

[2.] **C** doo. **Esus** Hearts are of-ten bro-ken **E/G#** when there are words un-spo-ken.

Am In your soul there's an-swers to your **Am/G** prayers. If you're

Dm7 search-ing for a place you know, a fa-mil-iar face, **C/E** some-where to go, you should

F look in-side your soul, you're half-way there. **Fmaj7/G** Some-times you'll

D.S. al Coda

CODA **C** doo.

DOO WOP
(That Thing)

Written by LAURYN HILL

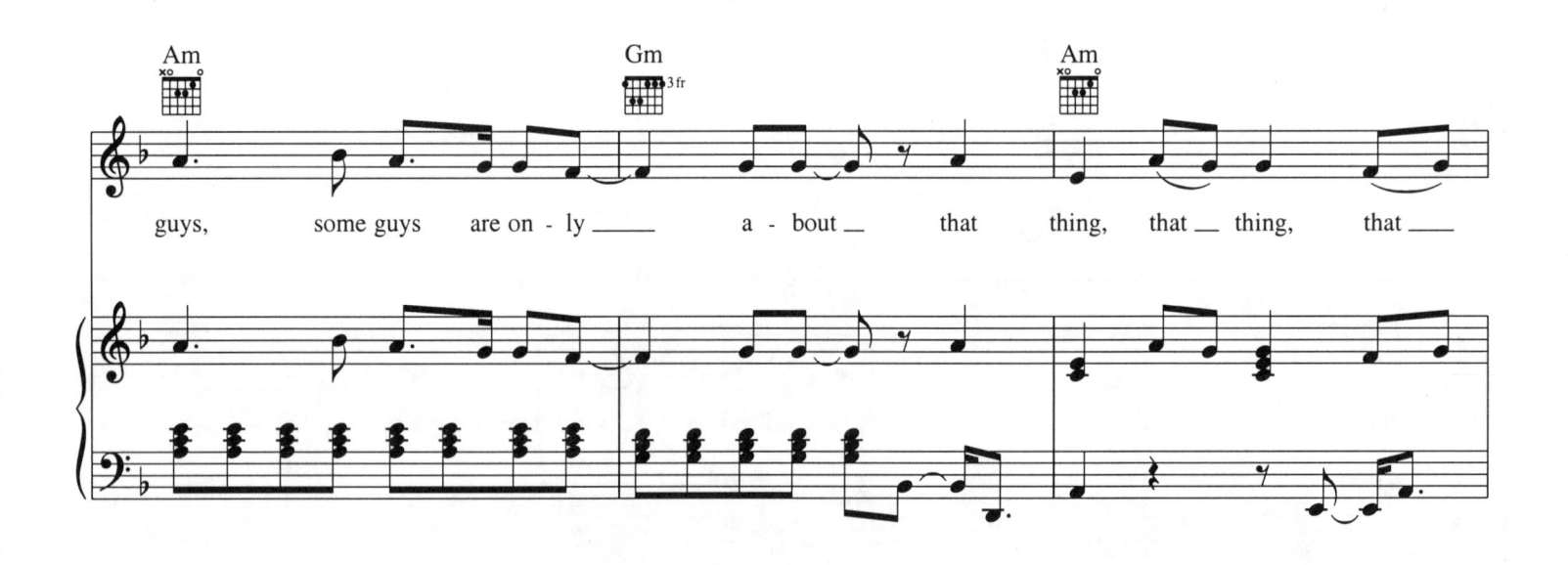

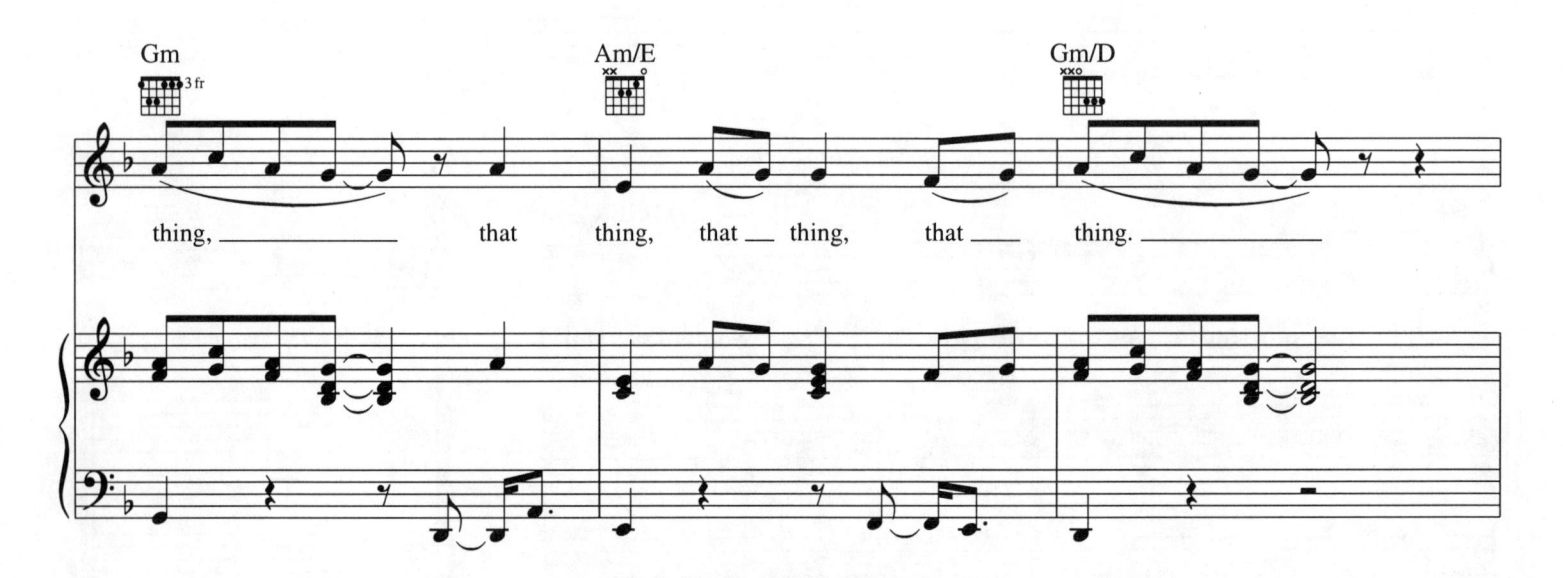

Yeah, yeah. Yeah, yeah. Yeah, yeah.

Yeah, yeah. Rap 1, 2 *(See additional lyrics)*

2, 3
Gm
B♭ Am Gm7/D Am
Gm
Am
Gm
N.C.
B♭ Am Gm7
Come a -
B♭ Am Gm
gain.
When, when, / Yo, yo,
come a - gain.
Freight train, come a - gain.
My friend, / N. C. string,
come a -

To Coda
B♭maj7 Am7 Gm7 Am Gm
3fr
gain. Yeah, yeah. Guys, you know you bet - ter watch out. Some
Am Gm Am
girls, some girls are on - ly a - bout that thing, that thing, that
D.S. al Coda
Gm Am Gm Gm/B♭ Am Gm/D
thing, that thing, that thing, that thing.
CODA
Am Gm
Watch out, watch out. Look out, look out.

Watch out, watch out. — Look out, look out. — Watch out, watch out. —

Look out, look out. — Watch out, watch out. — Look out, look out. —

Girls, you know you bet-ter — watch out. — Some guys, some guys are on-ly —

a-bout — that thing, that — thing, that — thing, — that

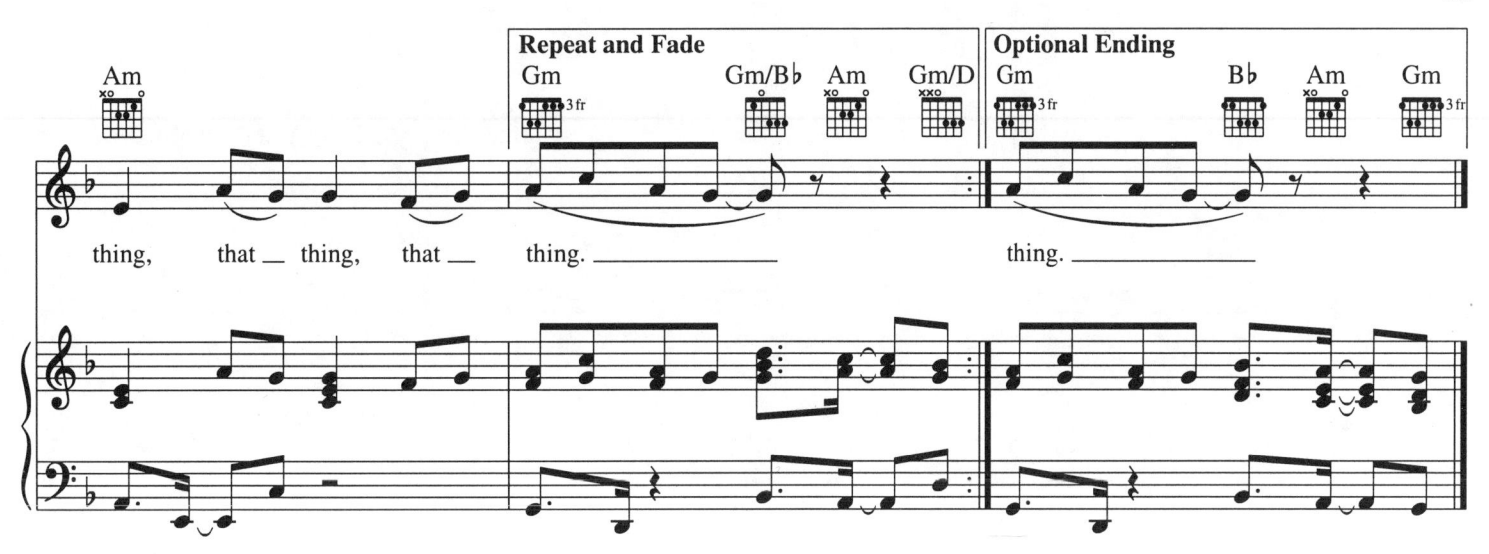

Additional Lyrics

Rap 1: It's been three weeks since you've been lookin' for your friend,
The one you let hit it and never called you again.
'Member when he told you he was 'bout the Benjamins.
You act like you ain't hear him, then give 'em a little trim.
To Begin, how you think you really gon' pretend?
Like you wasn't down, then you called him again.

Plus when, you give it up so easy you ain't even foolin' him.
If you did it then, then you probably fuck again.
Talkin' out your neck sayin' you're a Christian,
A Muslim sleepin' wit' the gin.
Now that was the sin that did Jezabel in.
Who you gon' tell when repercussion spin?

Showin' off your ass 'cause you're thinkin' it's a trend.
Girlfriend, let me break it down for you again.
You know I only say it 'cause I'm truly genuine.
Don't be a hard rock when you really a gem.
Baby girl, respect is just the minimum.
Niggas fucked up and you still defendin' 'em.

Now, Lauryn is only human.
Don't think I haven't been through the same predicament.
Let it sit inside your head like a million in Philly Penn.
It's silly when girls sell their souls because it's in. Look at where you bein.
Hair weaves like Europeans, fake nails done by Koreans.

Rap 2: The second verse is dedicated to the men
More concerned wit' his rims and his timbs than his women.
Him and his men come in the cub like hooligans.
Don't care who they defend, popping Yang like you got yen.

Let's not pretend,
They wanna pack pistol by they waist men.
Cristal by the case men, still they in they mother's basement.
The pretty face men claimin' that they did a bid men.
Need to take care of their three and four kids, men.

They facin' court case when the child support's late.
Money takin', heart breakin. Now you wonder why women hate men.
And the sneaky, silent men, the punk domestic violence men.
The quick to shoot the semen stop actin' like boys and be men.

How you gon' win when you ain't right within? *(3x's)*
Uh-uh, come again.

THE FIRST NIGHT

Words and Music by TAMARA SAVAGE, JERMAINE DUPRI, MARILYN McLEOD and PAMELA SAWYER

Original key: E♭ minor. This edition has been transposed down one half-step to be more playable.
*Vocal written one octave higher than sung.

© 1998 EMI APRIL MUSIC INC., MARSHAI PUBLISHING, SO SO DEF MUSIC and JOBETE MUSIC CO., INC.
All Rights Controlled and Administered by EMI APRIL MUSIC INC.
All Rights Reserved   International Copyright Secured   Used by Permission
- contains elements of "Love Hangover"

B♭/C
Dm
- pen, down to be o - pen for some sat - is - fac - tion? Did - n't wan - na say yes,
me. Want - ed to touch you, want - ed to kiss you and some - how in one
G
B♭/C
Dm
pray your re - ac - tion. I knew it was wrong for feel - in' this way,
night dis - cov - er I love you. Felt so right, but it felt so wrong.
G
B♭/C
es - pe - cially the thought of giv - in' in on the first date. Could - n't let go,
And look how you're car - ry - in' on, try - in' to say
Dm
G
it stayed on my mind. At the end of the night I had to de - cide.
things to get me to stay, but my watch tells me it's get - tin' too late.

Dm
I was think - in', I should make a move, but I won't. I know you're
I'm
G
Bb/C
Dm
pro - b'ly think - in' some-thin' is wrong, know - in' if I do that it won't be
G
Bb/C
right. I don't get down on the first night.
Dm
G
I should make a move, but I won't. I know you're pro - b'ly think - in' some-thin' is

wrong, know-in' if I do ___ that it won't be right. I wan-na get down, but not the first night. ___ night. ___ Oh, we're chill- ___ If you ___ want ___ me ___ you got ___ to know ___ me. ___ And if ___ you want ___ my ___ love ___

Asus
A
B♭maj7
C
you got - ta wait, my love. Ba - ba -
F
- by, that's the way it's got to be.
E♭
3 fr
Dm
A
Get to know me so we can do this.
Dm
G
I should make a move, but I won't. I know you're pro - b'ly think - in' some - thin' is
Lead vocal-ad lib.

wrong, know-in' if I do ___ that it won't be right. I don't get

down on the first night. I should make a move, but I won't. I know you're

pro-b'ly think-in' some-thin' is wrong, know-in' if I do ___ that it won't be right. I wan-na get

1,2 down, but not the first night. _____

3 down, but not the first night. _____

4 SEASONS OF LONELINESS

Words and Music by JAMES HARRIS III
and TERRY LEWIS

Flowing

I long for the warmth of days gone by

Original key: D♭ major. This edition has been transposed up one half-step to be more playable.

© 1997 EMI APRIL MUSIC INC. and FLYTE TYME TUNES INC.
All Rights Controlled and Administered by EMI APRIL MUSIC INC.
All Rights Reserved   International Copyright Secured   Used by Permission

F♯m7
G(add2)
D(add2)/F♯
when you were mine,
But now
Bm7
2 fr
E7sus
Em7/A
those days are mem - o - ries in time.
D
Bm7
2 fr
G(add2)
Life's emp - ty with - out you by my side.
Re - mem - ber the nights when we closed our eyes
F♯m7
G(add2)
F♯m7
Bm7(add4)
My heart be - longs to you no
and vowed that you and I would

mat - ter what ___ I try. ___ When I get the
be in love for all time. ___ An - y - time I

cour - age up to love some - bod - y new, ___ it al - ways falls a -
think a - bout these things I shared with you, ___ I break down and

part 'cause they just can't com - pare to you. ___ Your love won't re -
cry 'cause I get so e - mo - tion - al. ___ Un - til you re -

lease me, I'm bound un - der ball and chain, ___
lease me, I'm bound un - der ball and chain, ___ } rem - i - nisc - ing our love as I

watch four sea - sons (1.,2.) change.
(3.) gain.
(1.-3.) In comes the win - ter breeze that chills the air and drifts the snow.

And I i - mag - ine kiss - ing you un - der the mis - tle - toe. When spring - time makes its way here

li - lac blooms re - mind me of the scent of your ___ per - fume. ___

When sum - mer burns with heat I al - ways get the hots for you. Go skin - ny - dip - pin' in the

D/F♯
Bm7
G(add2)
D/F♯
Bm7
To Coda
o - cean where we used to do. When au - tumn sheds the leaves the trees are bare when you're not here. It
1
Cmaj7
Asus
does - n't feel the same.
Does - n't feel the same.
2
Cmaj7
A9sus
Bm
does - n't feel the same. This lone - li - ness
F♯7/A♯
Bm7/A
G♯m7♭5
has crushed my heart. Please let me love a - gain 'cause I need your

love to com-fort me and ease my pain, _____ or four sea-sons will bring the lone - li - ness a-

D.S. al Coda

CODA

does - n't feel ____ the same. __

Re - mem - ber the warmth of days __ gone by. _____

poco rit.

GET IT ON TONITE

Words and Music by MONTELL JORDAN, JORG EVANS,
JURGEN KORDULETSCH, DARREN BENBOW,
ANTOINE WILSON and BRIAN PALMER

When I'm looking at you I keep thinkin': Why can't she be like you? So I'm scheming. I can't go on like this, believing that her love is true. Standing on the

Copyright © 1999 by Famous Music Corporation, Montell Jordan Music, Warner-Tamerlane Publishing Corp.,
Tobaki, Inc., Levars Cribbe Music, Inc. and Chubby Music Publishing, Inc.
International Copyright Secured   All Rights Reserved
- contains a sample from "Love For The Sake Of Love" by Jorg Evans and Jurgen Korduletsch, published by Warner-Tamerlane Publishing Corp.

Fm
C7
dance floor while she's trick - in, you are all I want, girl. She's a chi -
Ebm
- cken. We might be to - geth - er, but love is miss - ing. Girl I want you,
Eb/Bb
F5/C
6fr
3fr
so what can we do? Girl, if its al - right
D.S. you.)
let's go some -
C7
where and get it on to - nite.
I've got a girl but you look good to - nite.
You should-n't have to be a - lone to - nite.

84

Tell me ba-by. Girl if you're rea-dy (I'm read-y.) we can get it on. (We can get it on.) I know where I went wrong. (She's where you went wrong.) With you is where I be-long. Girl, if I could find the words to say...

I've got-ta get a-way from a love that kills me ev-er-y day. (I'd glad-ly say to) Girl, if it's al- to-night.

87

E♭m
F/C
It's one on one to - nite, ___ to - nite. _
C7sus
Fm
___ Girl, if it's al - right... My ba - by's stress - in' me.
C7
E♭m
You need to come with me; we need to
F/C
C7sus
go some - where ___ to - nite, ___ to - nite. ___ Girl, if it's al -

right, let's go some-where and get it on to-nite.

I've got a girl but you look good to-nite.

It's one on one to-nite, ___ to-nite. ___ Girl, if it's al-right.

GETTIN' JIGGY WIT IT

*Words and Music by NILE RODGERS,
BERNARD EDWARDS, WILL SMITH,
SAMUEL J. BARNES and J. ROBINSON*

LOOP

Medium dance groove

LYRICS

Intro
(Loop)
Bring it.
Whoo!
Unh, unh, unh, unh
Hoo cah cah.
Hah hah, hah hah.
Bicka bicka bow bow bow,
Bicka bow bow bump bump.
What, what, what, what?
Hah hah hah hah.

Rap 1:
(Loop)
On your mark, ready, set, let's go.
Dance floor pro, I know you know
I go psycho when my new joint hit.
Just can't sit,
Gotta get jiggy wit it,
Ooh, that's it.
Now, honey, honey, come ride,
DKNY all up in my eye.
You gotta Prada bag with alotta stuff in it,
Give it to your friend, let's spin.
Everybody lookin' at me,
Glancin' the kid,
Wishin' they was dancin' a jig
Here with this handsome kid.
Ciga-cigar right from Cuba-Cuba,
I just bite it.
It's for the look, I don't light it.
Illway the an-may on the ance-day oor-flay,
Givin' up jiggy, make it feel like foreplay.
Yo, my car-dee-o is Infinit-
Ha, ha.
Big Willie Style's all in it,
Gettin' jiggy wit it.

Copyright © 1997 Sony/ATV Songs LLC, Warner-Tamerlane Publishing Corp., Bernard's Other Music,
Treyball Music, Slam U Well Music and Jelly's Jams, L.L.C.
All Rights on behalf of Sony/ATV Songs LLC Administered by Sony/ATV Music Publishing, 8 Music Square West, Nashville, TN 37203
International Copyright Secured   All Rights Reserved
- contains a sample of "He's The Greatest Dancer" written by Nile Rodgers and Bernard Edwards.
Copyright © 1978 Sony/ATV Songs LLC, Warner-Tamerlane Publishing Corp. and Bernard's Other Music

Refrain: Na na na na na na na, nana
(Loop) Na na na na nana.
Gettin' jiggy wit it.
(Repeat 3x)

Rap 2: What? You wanna ball with the kid?
(Loop) Watch your step, you might fall
Trying to do what I did.
Mama-unh, mama-unh, mama come closer
In the middle of the club with the rub-a-dub, uhn.
No love for the haters, the haters,
Mad cause I got floor seats at the Lakers.
See me on the fifty yard line with the Raiders.
Met Ali, he told me I'm the greatest.
I got the fever for the flavor of a crowd pleaser.
DJ, play another
From the prince of this.
Your highness,
Only mad chicks ride in my whips.
South to the west to the east to the north,
Bought my hits and watch 'em go off, a-go off.
Ah yes, yes y'all, ya don't stop.
In the winter or the (summertime),
I makes it hot
Gettin' jiggy wit 'em.

Refrain

Rap 3: Eight-fifty I.S.; if you need a lift,
(Loop) Who's the kid in the drop?
Who else, Will Smith,
Livin' that life some consider a myth.
Rock from South Street to One Two Fifth.
Women used to tease me,
Give it to me now nice and easy
Since I moved up like George and Wheezy.
Cream to the maximum, I be askin' 'em,
"Would you like to bounce with the brother that's platinum?"
Never see Will attackin' 'em,
Rather play ball with Shaq and um,
Flatten 'em,
Psyche.
Kiddin',
You thought I took a spill
But I didn't.
Trust the lady of my life, she hittin'.
Hit her with a drop top with the ribbon,
Crib for my mom on the outskirts of Philly.
You, trying to flex on me?
Don't be silly,
Gettin' jiggy wit it.

Refrain

HEARTBREAK HOTEL

Words and Music by TAMARA SAVAGE,
CARSTEN SCHACK and KENNETH KARLIN

Relaxed R&B groove

This is the Heart-break Ho- tel.__ This is the Heart-break Ho- tel.__ This is the Heart-break Ho- tel.__ This is the Heart-break Ho- tel.__ This is the Heart-break

Original key: E♭ minor. This edition has been transposed up one half-step to be more playable.

© 1998 EMI APRIL MUSIC INC., MARSHAI PUBLISHING, EMI BLACKWOOD MUSIC INC., JUNGLE FEVER MUSIC and SOULVANG MUSIC
All Rights for MARSHAI PUBLISHING Controlled and Administered by EMI APRIL MUSIC INC.
All Rights for JUNGLE FEVER MUSIC and SOULVANG MUSIC Controlled and Administered by EMI BLACKWOOD MUSIC INC.
All Rights Reserved   International Copyright Secured   Used by Permission

93

Am7
- ing not to cry
ask - ing my - self
that I wouldn't find out
that you were cheat-ing on
Em7
Am7
why
you do this to me, mmm,
me.
How could you do it to me?
F#m7b5
B7
ah, ba - by.
Since you're not a-round for me to tell you, ba - by, face
Em7
F#m7b5
to face,
I'm writ-ing you this let-ter and

[Sheet music]

do me right __ un-til you played with my e-mo-tions and you made me cry. __ What you do __ to me. Can't take what you did __ to me.

Now, I Heart-break Ho-tel. __ This is the Heart-break Ho-tel. __ This is the

Em7
G/A
Heart - break Ho - tel. This is the Heart - break
Em7
Ho - tel. This is the Heart - break Ho - tel. This is the
G/A
Em7
Heart - break Ho - tel. All I real - ly want - ed was some
Lead vocal - ad lib.
Am7
of your time. In - stead, you told me lies when some - one else was on your mind. What you do

to me. Look what you did ___ to me.

I thought that you were some-one who would do me right ___ un-til you played with my e-mo-tions and you made me cry. ___ What you do ___ to me.

Repeat and Fade

Optional Ending

Can't take what you did ___ to me.

HEARTBREAKER

Words and Music by MARIAH CAREY, JAY-Z,
SHIRLEY ELLISTON, LINCOLN CHASE,
NARADA MICHAEL WALDEN and JEFFREY COHEN

C
Am
gim - me your love, gim-me your love, gim-me your love, gim-me your love. Boy, your
uh huh. Whoo! Let's skate.)
C
Am
C
love's so good; I don't wan - na let go, and al - though I should, I can't
shame to be so eu - phor - ic and weak when you smile at me and you
Am
C
Am
leave you a - lone 'cause you're so dis - arm - ing. I'm caught up in the midst of you
tell me the things that you know per - suade me to re - lin - quish my love to you.
C
Am
C
and
But
I can - not re - sist at all.
(1., 2.) (Boy, if

I do the things you want me to, the way I used to do, would you love me ba - by, or leave me feel-ing used? Would you go and break my heart? Heart-break-er, you've got the best of me, but I just keep on com-ing back in - ces - sant - ly. Oh, why did you have to run your game on_me? I should have known right from the start you'd go_ and break my heart._

Gim-me your love, gim-me your love, gim-me your love, gim-me your love,

gim-me your love, gim-me your love, gim-me your love, gim-me your love. It's a

___ did you have to run your game on_me? I should have

Male, Spoken: I'm al-most read-y.

known right from the start you'd go __ and break my heart. __
O-kay,   cool.   All right   go.

Rap: *(See rap lyrics)*   *(Rap continues)*

Play 7 times

Heart-break-er, you've got the best of __ me but I just keep on com-ing back in-ces-sant-ly. Oh, __ why __ did you have to run your

Am
C
1
Am
game on _ me? I should have known right from the start you'd go _ and break my heart. _
C
2
Am
C
_ Heart-break-er, you've got the start you'd go _ and break my heart. _ Heart-break-er, you've got the
(Boy, if
Am
C
best of _ me, but I just keep on com-ing back in-
I do the things you want me to,
Am
C
ces-sant-ly. Oh, _ why _ did you have to run your
the way I used to do, would you love me,

game on me? I should have known right from the start you'd go and break my heart.
ba - by, or leave me feel-ing used? Would you go and...)

gim-me your love, gim-me your love, gim-me your love, gim-me your love.

Rap Lyrics

She wanna shout with Jay, play box with Jay.
She wanna pillow fight in the middle of the night.
She wanna drive my Benz with five of her friends.
She wanna creep past the block, spying again.
She wanna roll with Jay, chase skeeos away.
She wanna fight with lame chicks, blow my day.
She wanna respect the rest, kick me to the curb
If she find one strand of hair longer than hers.

She want love in the jacuzzi, rub up in the movies,
Access to the old crib, keys to the new, please.
She wanna answer the phone, tattoo her arm.
That's when I gotta send her back to her mom.
She call me "heartbreaker." When we apart, it makes her
Want a piece of paper, scribble down "I hate ya."
But she knows she love Jay, because
She love everything Jay say, Jay does, and uh,...

I GET LONELY

Words and Music by TERRY LEWIS, JAMES HARRIS III,
JANET JACKSON and RENE ELIZONDO JR.

Slow R&B ballad

you. I get so lone-ly. I can't let just an-y-bod-y hold me. You are the one that lives in me, my dear.

© 1997 EMI APRIL MUSIC INC., Flyte Tyme Tunes Inc. and Black Ice Publishing
All Rights for Flyte Tyme Tunes Inc. Controlled and Administered by EMI April Music Inc.
All Rights Reserved   International Copyright Secured   Used by Permission

Gm9 Fmaj9 Em9 A7#5(♭9) Dm7
I want no one but you. I get so
Cm9 F7 B♭maj7 A7 A7/C# Dm7
lonely I can't let just any-body hold me.
You are
G7 Cm9 F7 B♭maj7
the one that lives in me, my dear. I
To Coda
Gm9 Fmaj9 Em9 A7#5(♭9) Dm9 Cm9 F7 B♭maj7
want no one but... Sit-ting here with my tears,
I still re-mem-ber to the day,

G/A A7/C# Dm7 G7
I'm all a - lone with my fears. I'm won - der - ing if I have
in fact it was a third Mon - day you came a - long to be
Cm7 F7 B♭maj7 Gm9 Fmaj9 Em9 A7#5(♭9)
to do with - out 'cha, but there's no rea - son
the one for me and now I'm so a - lone.
Dm7 Cm7 F7 B♭maj7
why. I fell a - sleep late last night cry - ing like a
I'm sit - ting here by the phone. Call to say that
G/A A7#5/C# Dm7 G7 Cm7 F6 B♭maj7
new born child, hold - ing my - self close, pre - tend - ing my arms are yours.
you're o - kay so that I'll have a chance to beg you to stay.

1
2
D.S. al Coda
Gm9 Fmaj9 Em9 A7#5(b9)
Gm9 Fmaj9 Em9 A7#5(b9)
I want no one but
I want no one but
CODA
Dm Cm7 F7 Bbmaj7
you. Ev - 'ry - time I see your face, ba - by, ev - 'ry - time I
A7 A7/C# Dm7 G7 Cm9 F7 Bbmaj7
hear your name, I do be - lieve that you and me are no
You're all the love that lives in me, babe.
Gm9 Fmaj9 Em9 A7#5(b9) Dm7
long - er. I want no one but
Gon-na

Cm7 F7 B♭maj7 A7sus A7/C♯ Dm7
break it down, break it down, break it down. Gon-na break it down, break it down,
G7 Cm7 F7 B♭maj7
break it down. Whoa.
Gm9 C/F D/E A7♯5(♭9) Dm7 Cm7 F7 B♭maj7
You know that I know that I
A7sus A7/C♯ Dm7 G7 Cm9 F7
get so lone-ly. Love you, hoo hoo. No,

111

I'LL BE MISSING YOU

Written and Composed by
STING

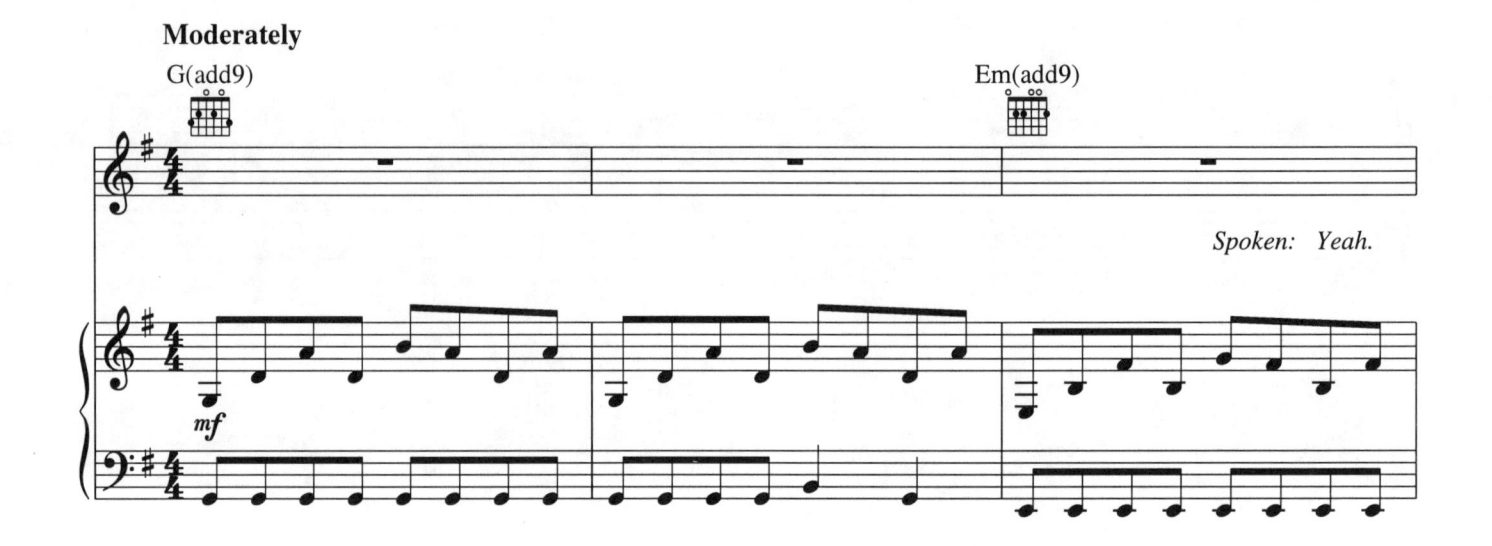

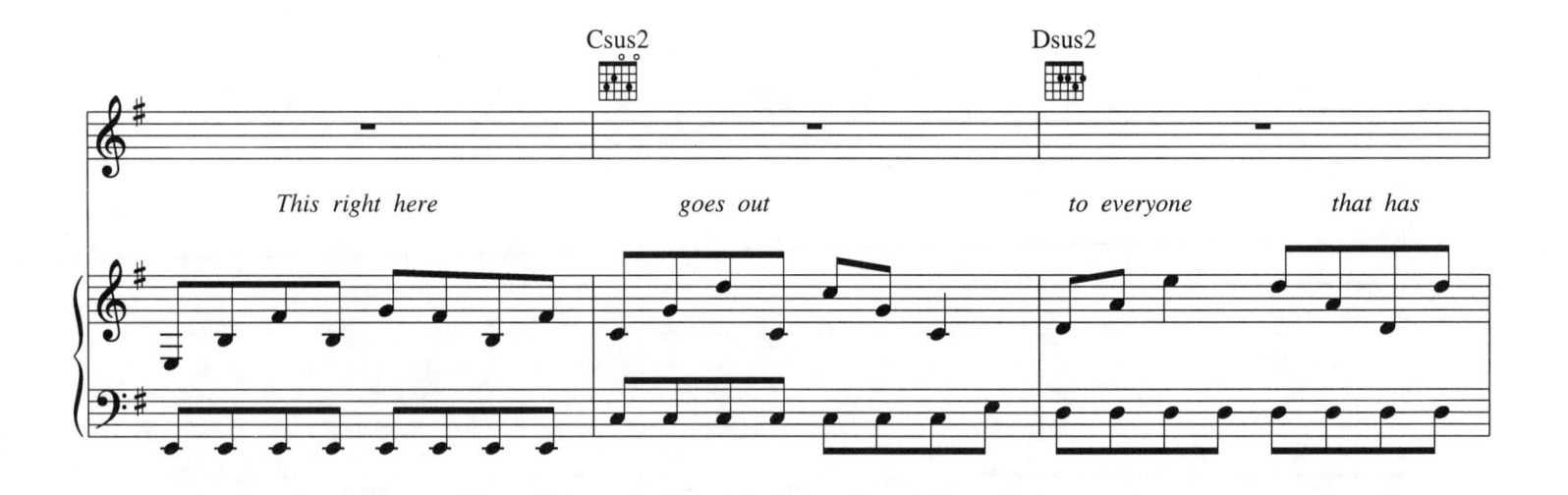

Moderately

Spoken: Yeah.

This right here goes out to everyone that has lost someone that they truly love. Check it out.

Rap 1:
Rap 2:
Rap 3:
Rap 4:
(See rap lyrics)

© 1997 G.M. SUMNER
Published by MAGNETIC PUBLISHING LTD. and Administered by EMI BLACKWOOD MUSIC INC. in the USA and Canada
All Rights Reserved   International Copyright Secured   Used by Permission

Em(add9)
Csus2
Dsus2
G(add9)
1, 3
2, 4
Sung: Ev - 'ry step I take,
Em(add9)
ev - 'ry move I make,
ev - 'ry sin - gle day,

[Csus2] ev-'ry time I pray [Dsus2] I'll be miss-ing [G(add9)] you.

Think-ing of the day when you went a-[Em(add9)]way, what a life to take, [Csus2] what a bond to break.

[Dsus2] I'll be miss-ing [G(add9)] you.

To Coda ⊕

D.S. al Coda

CODA

Some-bod-y tell me why.

On that morn-ing, when this life is o-ver, I know I'll see your face.

Ev-'ry night I pray, ev-'ry step I take,

Em(add9)
ev - 'ry move I make, ev - 'ry sin - gle day. Ev - 'ry night I pray,
Csus2
Dsus2
1
G(add9)
ev - 'ry step I take, ev - 'ry move I make, make. ev - 'ry sin - gle day.
2
G(add9)
Ev - 'ry night I pray, We miss you. Ev - 'ry step I
Em(add9)
(1., 3.) take, ev - 'ry move I make,
(2., 4.) day when you went a - way,

ev - 'ry sin - gle day, ev - 'ry time I pray
what a life to take, what a bond to break.

I'll be miss - ing you.
I'll be miss - ing you.

Repeat and Fade

Think-ing of the
Ev - 'ry step I

Rap Lyrics

Rap 1: Seems like yesterday we used to rock the show.
I laced the track, you locked the flow.
So far from hangin' on the block for dough.
Notorious, they got to know that life ain't always what it
Seemed to be. Words can't express what you mean to me.
Even though you're gone, we still a team.
Through your family, I'll fulfill your dreams.

Rap 2: In the future, can't wait to see if you open up the gates for me.
Reminisce sometime the night they took my friend.
Try to black it out, but it plays again.
When it's real, feelin's hard to conceal.
Can't imagine all the pain I feel.
Give anything to hear half your breath.
I know you're still livin' your life after death.

Rap 3: It's kinda hard with you not around. Know you're in heaven smilin' down
Watchin' us while we pray for you.
Ev'ry day we pray for you.
Till the day we meet again, in my heart is where I keep you, friend.
Memories give me the strength I need to proceed,
Strength I need to believe.

Rap 4: My thoughts, Big, I just can't define.
Wish I could turn back the hands of time,
Us and a six, shop for new clothes and kicks,
You and me take in flicks.
Make a hit, stages they receive you on.
Still can't believe you're gone.
Give anything to hear half your breath.
I know you're still livin' your life after death.

IT'S NOT RIGHT BUT IT'S OKAY

Words and Music by LaSHAWN DANIELS, RODNEY JERKINS, FRED JERKINS, TONI ESTES and ISAAC PHILLIPS

Moderate Dance beat

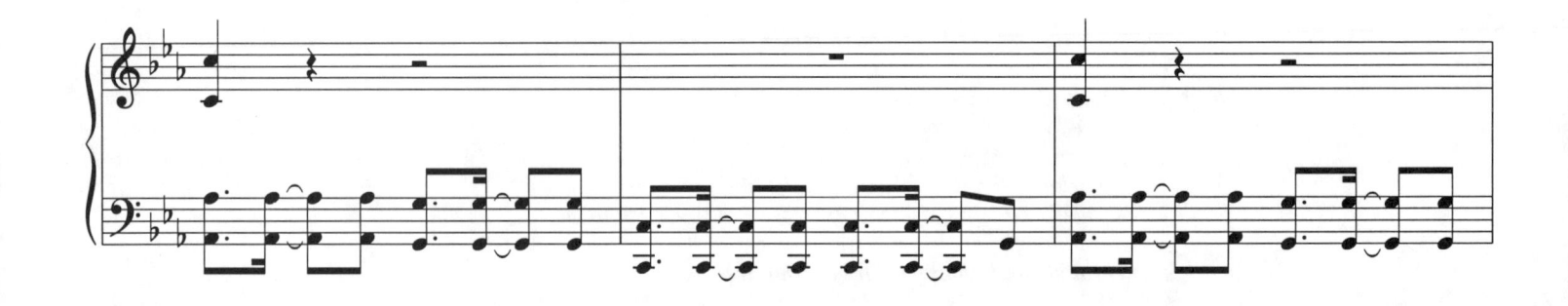

Fri-day

© 1998 EMI APRIL MUSIC INC., LASHAWN DANIELS PRODUCTIONS INC., EMI BLACKWOOD MUSIC INC., RODNEY JERKINS PRODUCTIONS INC., FRED JERKINS PUBLISHING, ENSIGN MUSIC CORPORATION, UNIVERSAL - MCA MUSIC PUBLISHING, A Division of UNIVERSAL STUDIOS, INC., MIC'L MUSIC and PINK JEANS PUBLISHING
All Rights for LASHAWN DANIELS PRODUCTIONS INC. Controlled and Administered by EMI APRIL MUSIC INC.
All Rights for RODNEY JERKINS PRODUCTIONS INC. Controlled and Administered by EMI BLACKWOOD MUSIC INC.
All Rights for MIC'L MUSIC Controlled and Administered by UNIVERSAL - MCA MUSIC PUBLISHING, A Division of UNIVERSAL STUDIOS, INC.
All Rights Reserved   International Copyright Secured   Used by Permission

night you and your boys went out to eat. Ah.
bags so you can leave town for a week. Yes, I am.

Then they hung out, but you came home a-round
The phone rings, and then you look at me.

three. Yes, you did. If six of
You said it

y'all went out, uh, then
was one of your friends

Gm7
3fr
Ab
4fr
four of you are real - ly cheap. Yeah. 'Cause on - ly
down on fif - ty fourth street, boy. So
Cm
3fr
Bb
Gm7
3fr
two of you had din - ner; I found your cre - dit card re - ceipt.
why did 2 1 3 show up on your call - er I. D.?
Ab
4fr
N.C.
It's not right, but it's o - kay. I'm gon - na
make it an - y way. Pack your bags up and

leave. Don't you dare come running back to me. It's not

right, but it's o-kay. I'm gon-na make it an-y

way. Close the door be-hind you, leave your key. I'd rath-er be a-

lone than un-hap-py. Yeah. Ah. Ah.

122

Ah. Yeah ah. I'm pack-in'

py, _____ yeah. _____ I have been ___ through ___ all of this be - fore. I've been through

all this be - fore. So how ___ could you think _____ Don't

think a - bout ___ it, don't think a - bout ___ it. that I would stand a - round _____ and take some more?

Cm
Things are gon - na change.
Get gone, get gone.
Fm
'Cause I won't be a fool an - y - more.
Things are gon - na change, ba - by. You don't
Cm
That's why you have to leave.
stand no chance, boy. I say
Fm7
So don't turn a - round to see my face.
yeah yeah yeah yeah yeah. Don't you turn a -

round.___ There's no more tears left here for_ you to see. Was it real-ly worth you go-ing out like that? Tell me, boy.___ Was it real-ly worth you go-ing out like that? See I'm_ mov-ing on___

and I re-fuse to turn back, yeah.

See, all of this time

I thought I had some-bod-y down for with me.

It turns out

you were mak-ing a fool ___ of ___ me, ah. ___

___ Oh. ___

D.S. al Coda

It's not

CODA

py, oh ___ oh.

IT'S SO HARD TO SAY GOODBYE TO YESTERDAY

Words and Music by FREDDIE PERREN
and CHRISTINE YARIAN

Slowly

How do I say good-bye to what we had?
know where this road is going to lead.

The good times that made us laugh out-weighed the
All I know is where we've been and what we've

bad. I thought we'd get to see for-
been through. If we get to see to-

© 1975 JOBETE MUSIC CO., INC.
All Rights Controlled and Administered by EMI APRIL MUSIC INC.
All Rights Reserved   International Copyright Secured   Used by Permission

ev - er, _____ but for - ev - er's gone a -
mor - row, _____ I hope it's worth all __ the

way.
pain. } It's so hard _____ to say good-bye _____ to yes - ter - day. ____

I don't ____ And I'll take _____ with me the

mem - o - ries _____ to be my sun - shine af - ter the rain. ____ It's so hard _____ to say __ good-bye _____ to yes-ter-day. __

And I'll rain. __

It's so hard _____ to say __ good-bye __

__ to yes-ter-day. __

MY WAY

Words and Music by JERMAINE DUPRI, MANUEL SEAL and USHER RAYMOND

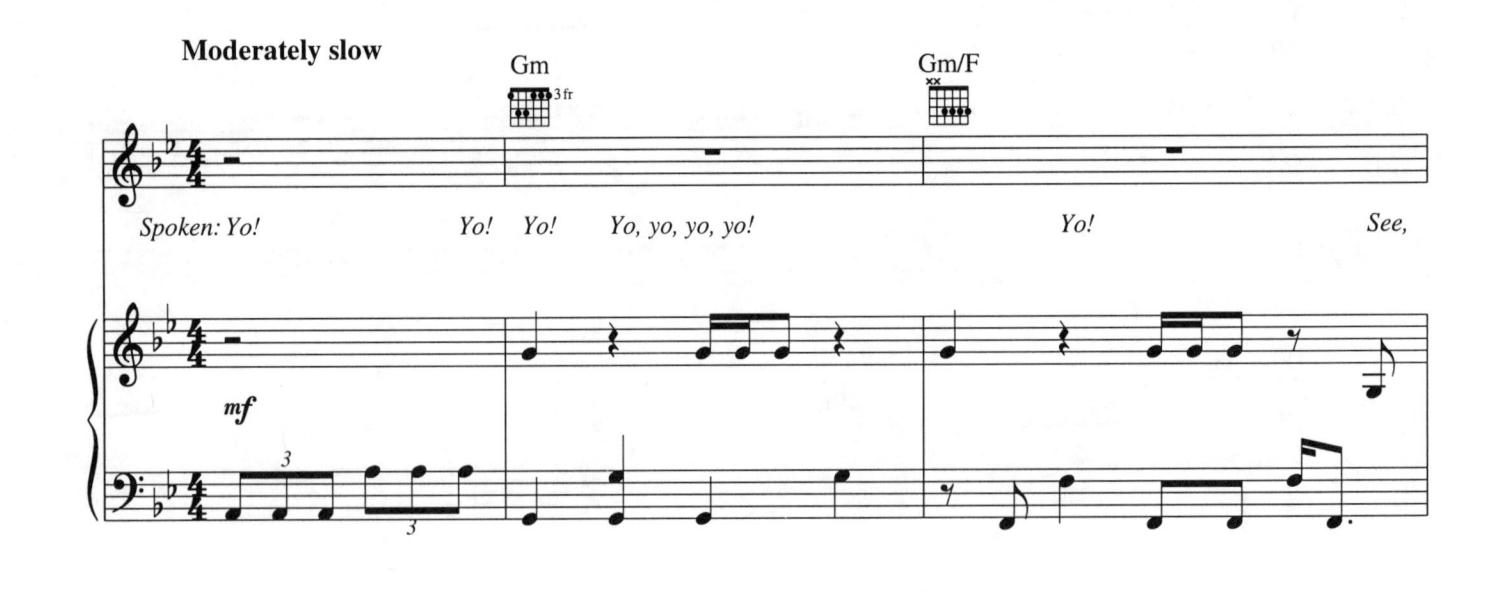

Moderately slow

Spoken: Yo! Yo! Yo! Yo, yo, yo, yo! Yo! See, it's rare that you find people like us, heh, 'cause all your other look out there doing what I'm doing, or trying to do what I'm doing. But you can't, 'cause I do what I do my way. What about you? Huh? Huh? C'mon!

© 1997 EMI APRIL MUSIC INC., SO SO DEF MUSIC, UR-IV MUSIC, BMG SONGS, INC. and SLACK A.D. MUSIC
All Rights for SO SO DEF MUSIC and UR-IV MUSIC Controlled and Administered by EMI APRIL MUSIC INC.
All Rights for SLACK A.D. MUSIC Administered by BMG SONGS, INC.
All Rights Reserved   International Copyright Secured   Used by Permission

131

-is-fy__ her need;__ she_ keeps run-ning back_ to see_ me do-ing it my way, my way. And what I say goes,__ and I'm in con-trol.___

Rap: (see additional lyrics)

D.S. al Coda

CODA Gm   Gm/F

Don't check me.   It was your girl who   let me   take it this far,   then, *whoo - ee, she had to have it ev-'ry chance that she could get. What you think, you were ball-er? 'N' I'm gon' call her. Clip that. You can get mad if you want to. Say what-ev-er you want, but she's still gon-na give it up. She likes it my way, my way. You can't sat-is-fy her need; she keeps run-*

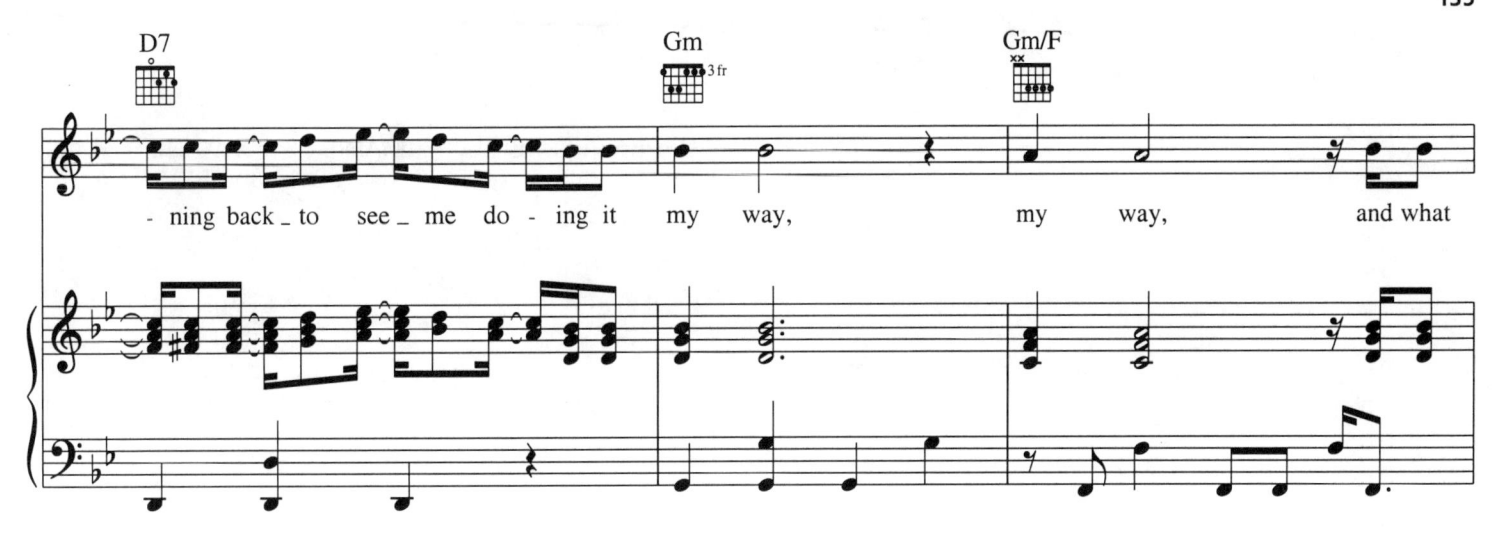

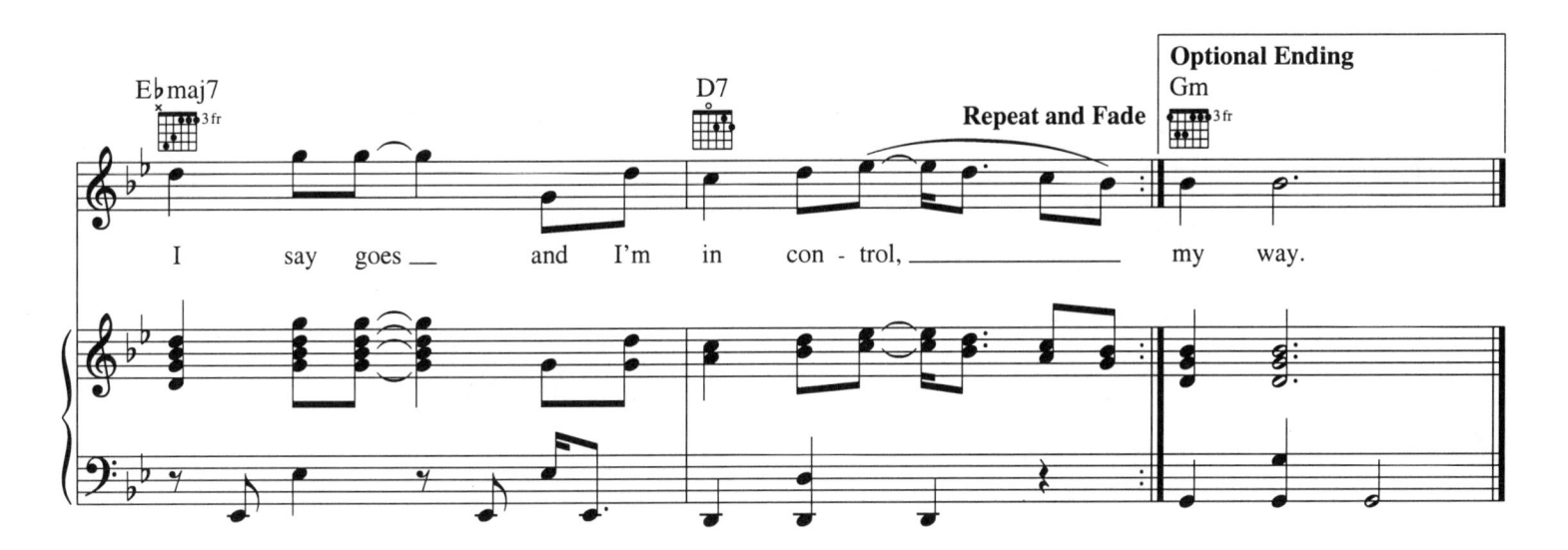

Additional Lyrics

Bad ass senoritas, two-seaters for kicks.
New kicks, it's all in the mix.
Don't turn no tricks, they turn for me.
Catching bricks don't concern me, so forget it, little midget.

My mind doing seven digits.
Before I pay, heaven and skies to visit.
Now dig it. I'm pulling all stops, locking down all spots,
Saying you can't front.

So from this day forth, you know I'm all about heat,
And what I do be the major league.
That's why your girlfriend's paging me.
'Cause she know like he know,
You don't see her like I see her,
So she's out the door.

Shotgun in my drop, havin' fun with the
Dumb system, based on conversation
About how she been chasing me and
Facing me, saying, "Give it to me now, baby."

NICE & SLOW

Words and Music by JERMAINE DUPRI, MANUEL SEAL,
USHER RAYMOND and BRIAN CASEY

Slowly

Spoken: Whatcha doing? Really? You know I'm coming over, right? Now you got it hot for me already, baby? Okay.
(Now baby, tell me what you wanna do with me.)
Be there by, uh, give me ten minutes. Be ready. Hey, wear that little thing I like. *Sung:* It's sev-en o-clock
(Now baby, tell me what you want to do with me.)

© 1997 EMI APRIL MUSIC INC., SO SO DEF MUSIC, UR-IV MUSIC, BMG SONGS, INC., SLACK A.D. MUSIC and THEM DAMN TWINS
All Rights for SO SO DEF MUSIC and UR-IV MUSIC Controlled and Administered by EMI APRIL MUSIC INC.
All Rights for SLACK A.D. MUSIC Administered by BMG SONGS, INC.
All Rights Reserved   International Copyright Secured   Used by Permission

137

take you to a place real nice and qui-et. There ain't no one there to in-ter-rupt, ain't got-ta rush.

I just wan-na take it nice and slow.
Spoken: (Now baby, tell me what you wanna do with me.)
See, I been

wait-ing for this for so long, we'll be mak-in' love un-til the sun comes up. Ba-by,

I just wan-na take it nice and slow. (1.) Now here we are
Spoken: (Now baby, tell me what you wanna do with me.) (2.) Now

driv-in' 'round town, con-tem-plat-ing where I'm gon-na lay you down. Girl, you've got me say-ing

my, my, my, I wish that I could pull o - ver and get this thing start-ed right now.

I wan-na do some-thing freak-y to you, babe. I don't think they heard me.

I wan-na do some-thing freak-y to you, babe, so call out my name.

Rap: (See Rap lyrics)

Let me tell me, do you wan-na get freak-y? 'Cause I'll freak you right, I will. I'll freak you right, I will. I'll freak you like no one has ev-er, ev-er made you feel.

Spoken: Now baby, tell me what you wanna do with me.

Lyrics under music: I'll freak you right, I will. I'll freak you right, I will. I'll freak you, freak you like no one has ev-er made you feel, yeah.

Repeat and Fade

OPTIONAL ENDING

Rap Lyrics

They call me U-s-h-e-r R-a-y-m-o-n-d.
Now baby, tell me what you wanna do with me.
Gotta nigga feenin' like Jodeci
Every time that you roll with me, holding me,
Trying to keep control of me nice and slowly.
You know never letting go, never lessen up the flow.
This is how the hook go, come on.

NO MATTER WHAT
from WHISTLE DOWN THE WIND

Music by ANDREW LLOYD WEBBER
Lyrics by JIM STEINMAN

Moderately slow

No matter what they tell us, no matter what they do,
no matter what they teach us, what we believe is true.

If only tears were laughter, if only night was day,
if only prayers were answered then we would hear God say.

© Copyright 1996, 1998 The Really Useful Group Ltd., Universal - Songs Of PolyGram International, Inc. and Lost Boys Music
All Rights for The Really Useful Group Ltd. in the United States and Canada Administered by Universal - PolyGram International Publishing, Inc.
International Copyright Secured   All Rights Reserved

A
No mat - ter what they call us, how - ev - er they at -
No mat - ter what they tell you, no mat - ter what they
Bm/A
Bm
D/E
E
tack, no mat - ter where they take us,
do, no mat - ter what they teach you,
Esus
E
A
we'll find our own way back.
what you be - lieve is true.
I can't de - ny what I
And I will keep you safe
A7
D
be - lieve, I can't be what I'm not.
and strong and shel - tered from the storm.

| Bm | D/E E | Esus E7 |

I know our love's for - ev - er, I know no mat - ter what.
No mat - ter where it's bar - ren our dream is be - ing born.

1. A
2. A | C

| Dm |

| Dm/G G7 | G | C |

F/C C Dm
No mat-ter who they fol - low, no mat-ter where they lead,
F/G G7 Gsus G7
no mat - ter how they judge us I'll be ev - 'ry one you need.
C C7/E
No mat - ter if the sun don't shine,
F C/E Dm
or if the skies are blue. No mat - ter what the

F/G
G7
Gsus
3 fr
G7
C
end - ing, my life be - gan with you. I
C7/E
F
C/E
can't de - ny what I be - lieve, I can't be what I'm not.
rit.
Slower
Dm7
G7
I know this love's for - ev - er, That's all that mat - ters now no mat - ter
Tempo I
C
Repeat and Fade
No no mat - ter no. No no mat - ter no.
what. No no mat - ter what. No no mat -

ON AND ON

Words and Music by ERICA WRIGHT and JAMAL CANTERO

Funky beat

Oh, my my my. I'm feelin' high. My money's gone. I'm all alone. Too much to see. The world keeps turnin'. Oh, what a day. What a day, what a day. The

Copyright © 1997 by BMG Songs, Inc., Tribes Of Kedar, Divine Pimp Publishing, Songs Of Universal, Inc. and McNooter Music
All Rights for Tribes Of Kedar and Divine Pimp Publishing Administered by BMG Songs, Inc.
All Rights for McNooter Music Controlled and Administered by Songs Of Universal, Inc.
International Copyright Secured   All Rights Reserved

Peace and blessin's' man-i-fest with ev-'ry les-son learned.
man that knows some-thing knows that he knows noth-ing at all. Does it seem
rush in-to de-struc-tion 'cause you don't have noth-in' left. The

If your know-ledge were your wealth, then it would be well-earned.
cold-er in your sum-mer-time and hot-ter in your fall?
moth-er ship can't save you, so your ass is gon-na get left. If

we were made in His im-age, then call us by our names. Most in-tel-

lects do not be-lieve in God, but they fear us just the same. Oh,

149

150

Lyrics:
I _____ was born un-der wat-er with _ three dol-lars and six dimes. Yeah, you _ may laugh _ 'cause you did not do your math. _ Like one two _ three. Damn, you all feel that? Like one two _ three.

2. Mad props to the god Ja-Borne. _ I _____ am feel-in' kind of hun-gry

[Cmaj9] 'cause my high is comin' down. [B7] [Em] Don't feed me yours [Em7/D]

[Cmaj9] 'cause your food does not endure. [B7] [Em] I think I need a cup of tea. [Em7/D]

[Cmaj9] The world keeps burnin'. [B7] [Em] Oh, what a day. [Em7/D]

[Cmaj9] What a day, what a day. [B7] You

D.S. al Coda

CODA [B7#5] [Em9] On ___ and on and on.

NO SCRUBS

*Words and Music by KANDI L. BURRUSS,
TAMEKA COTTLE and KEVIN BRIGGS*

Original key: G# minor. This edition has been transposed down one half-step to be more playable.

© 1999 EMI APRIL MUSIC INC., AIR CONTROL MUSIC, KANDACY MUSIC, TINY TAM MUSIC, SHEK'EM DOWN MUSIC, HITCO-MUSIC SOUTH and TONY MERCEDES MUSIC
All Rights for AIR CONTROL MUSIC, KANDACY MUSIC and TINY TAM MUSIC Controlled and Administered by EMI APRIL MUSIC INC.
All Rights Reserved   International Copyright Secured   Used by Permission

Gm
D7
G5
what he wants and just sits on his broke ass.
look - in' like trash. Can't get wit' a dead beat ass.
So,
Cm7
Gm
D7
no, I don't want your num - ber. No, I don't wan - na
Gm
Cm7
Gm
D7
give you mine and no, I don't wan - na meet you no - where. No, don't want
G5
Cm7
Gm
D7
none of your time and no, I don't want no scrub. A scrub is a guy that can't
3 fr

154

try'n to hol-ler at me. If you don't have a car and you're walk-in', oh, yes, son, I'm talk-in' to you. If you live at home wit' your ma-ma, oh, yes, son, I'm talk-in' to you. If you have as-sured me that you don't show love, oh, yes, son, I'm

Gm7
3 fr
C7
talk - in' to you. Wan - na get with me with no mon - ey, oh
F9sus
D7/F#
Cm7
3 fr
no, I don't want no...
No
Gm
3 fr
D7
Gm
3 fr
scrub.
Cm7
3 fr
Gm
3 fr
D7
G5
3 fr
No
scrub.
No, no.

157

NOBODY

Words and Music by FITZGERALD SCOTT
and KEITH SWEAT

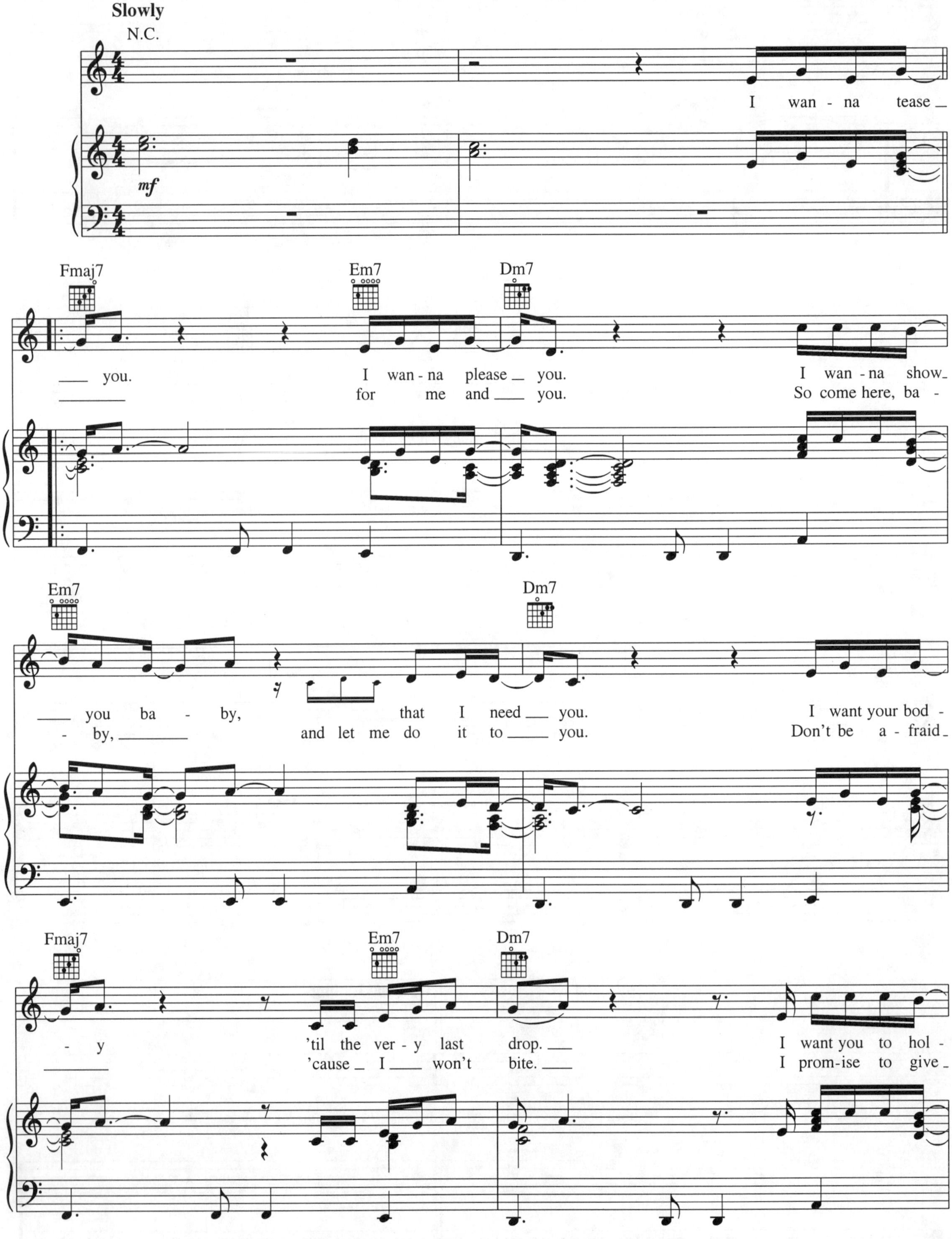

Em7
Dm7
- ler when you want me to stop.
it to you just the way you like.
And who can love you like
Fmaj7
Em7
Dm7
(No-bod - y, no-bod - y,
me? Who can sex you like me?
Who can treat you like me,
Who can lay your bod -
Em7
Dm7
no-bod - y, no-bod - y.
my ba - by?
- y down?
No - bod - y, ba - by.
And who can do it like
And who can treat you like
Fmaj7
Em7
Dm7
No-bod - y, no-bod - y,
me?
me?
Who can give you what you need?
Who can do you all

1
2
Em7
Dm7
Fmaj7
no-bod - y,
no-bod - y.)
night long?
No - bod - y, ba - by.
I want the night
no-bod - y.)
- by, and the band keeps play-in' on.
Bow wow wohn-in - on wohn,
bow wow wohn-in - on wohn,
bow wow wohn-in - on wohn.
No-bod - y, ba - by.
I want you right now for my lov -
(And may - be I...)

Em7
Dm7
er. Place no one a - bove ya. If you need
Fmaj7
Em7
Dm7
5
a love, I'll be right there, I'll be right there, ba - by, if it hurts me to love ya,
(If you need my love, I'll come run - nin', oh ba -
Em7
Dm7
Fmaj7
Em7
ba - by. Oh, yes, I will. Oh, yes, I will, ba - by.
- by. Yes, I will.)
Lead vocal ad lib.
(No - bod - y,
Dm7
Em7
Dm7
Repeat and Fade
no - bod - y, no - bod - y, no - bod - y, but me.)

SATISFY YOU

Words and Music by SEAN "PUFFY" COMBS, ROGER GREENE,
KELLY PRICE, R. KELLY, JEFF WALKER, JAY KING,
DENZIL FOSTER and THOMAS McELROY

Original key: B♭ minor. This edition has been transposed up one half-step to be more playable.

© 1999 EMI APRIL MUSIC INC., JUSTIN COMBS PUBLISHING COMPANY, INC., EMI BLACKWOOD MUSIC INC.,
JANICE COMBS PUBLISHING, INC., THELMA'S BOI PUBLISHING, SONY/ATV TUNES LLC, DUB'S WORLD MUSIC, SONGS OF UNIVERSAL, INC.,
PRICE IS RIGHT MUSIC, R. KELLY PUBLISHING, INC., LEHSEM SONGS and TWO TUFF ENUFF PUBLISHING
All Rights for JUSTIN COMBS PUBLISHING COMPANY, INC. Controlled and Administered by EMI APRIL MUSIC INC.
All Rights for JANICE COMBS PUBLISHING, INC. and THELMA'S BOI PUBLISHING Controlled and Administered by EMI BLACKWOOD MUSIC INC.
All Rights for SONY/ATV TUNES LLC and DUB'S WORLD MUSIC Administered by SONY/ATV MUSIC PUBLISHING, 8 Music Square West, Nashville, TN 37203
All Rights for R. KELLY PUBLISHING, INC. Administered by ZOMBA SONGS, INC.
All Rights for LEHSEM SONGS Administered by MUSIC & MEDIA INTERNATIONAL
All Rights Reserved   International Copyright Secured   Used by Permission
- contains elements of "Why You Treat Me So Bad"

CHORUS

He don't un-der-stand you like I do.

No, he'll nev-er make love to you like I do. So, give it to me

'cause I could show you 'bout a real love and I can

promise an-y-thing that I do is just to sat-is-fy you.

BRIDGE

Don't let him sing you a sad song too long. All that you
wait-ing for love like this

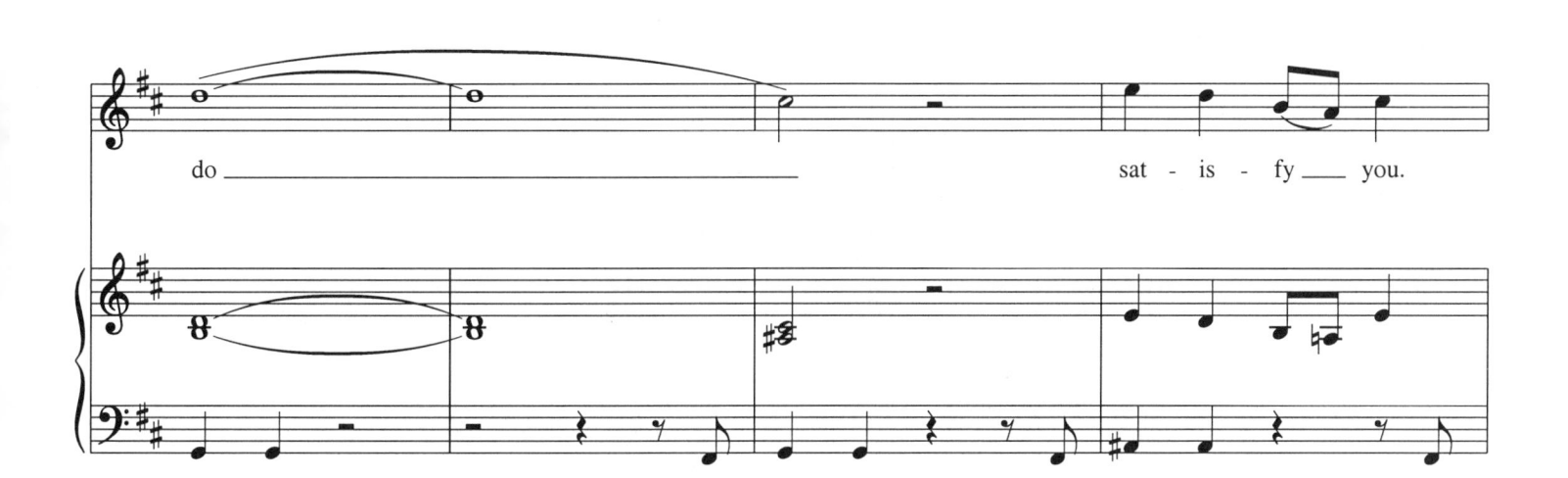

LYRICS

Intro: *(Spoken:)* All I want is somebody who's gon' love me
(Loop) for me, somebody I could love for them. All this money don't mean shit if you ain't got nobody to share it with. Love rules the world. You feel me?

Chorus:

Rap 1: When it hurt, I ease the pain, girl, caress your frame.
(Loop) Get them worries off your brain, girl. I'm in your corner.
Do what you want. It's your thing, girl.
I'll persist and try, but we one in the same, girl.
It ain't a game. So, I can't play wit you. I wanna lay wit you,
stay wit you, pray wit you, grow old and grey wit you.
In good and bad times, we'll always make it through
'Cause what we got is true, no matter what they say to you.
(Sung: Ooh, can I be your baby?*)*
I could straight-lace you, not just appearance,
Stimulate your mind, strengthen your spirits,
Be the voice of reason when you ain't try'n to hear it.
You want it, but you fear it, but you love it when you near it.
(Sung: Ooh, treat you like a lady.*)*
Sittin' on the sofa, gettin' to me closer.
Touch you right. Do it like a man's supposed ta.
Knew you was the one, that's why I chose ya
'Cause you get down for yours and ride like a soldier.

Chorus:

Rap 2:   Your soul ain't a toy, you ain't dealin' wit a boy,
(Loop)   Feel emptiness inside? I can feel that void.
                 When you spend time wit your woman and listen,
                 It shines more than any baguette diamond can glisten.
                 I can't impress you wit the cars and the wealth
                 'Cause any woman wit will and drive can get it herself.
                 I'd rather show you it's heartfelt, make your heart melt
                 And prove to you you're more important than anything else.
                 (Sung: Ooh, can I be your baby?*)*
                 Worthwhile, special like my first child.
                 When I see your face, it's always like the first time
                 Our eyes met. I knew we be together in a trijet.
                 I wanna give you things that I didn't buy yet.
                 (Sung: Ooh, treat you like a lady.*)*
                 Hold you, mold you. Don't know? Let me show you.
                 Ain't no tellin' what we could grow to.
                 Let it be known I told you.
                 And I'm 'a be there for whatever you go through.
                 My love is true.

Chorus:

Bridge:

Rap 3:   I'm that light when you can't see.
(Loop)   I'm that air when you can't breathe.
                 I'm that feelin' when you can't leave.
                 Some doubt, some believe. Some lie, cheat, and deceive.
                 So, it's only you and me. When you weak, I'll make you strong.
                 Here's where you belong. I ain't perfect, but I promise
                 I won't do you wrong. Keep you 'way from harm.
                 My love is protected. I'll wrap you in my arms so you never feel neglected.
                 I'll just make you aware of what we have is rare.
                 In the moment of despair, I'm the courage when you scared.
                 Loyal, down for you, soon as I saw you
                 Wanted to be there 'cause I could hold it down for you,
                 Be around for you. Plant seeds in the soil.
                 Make love all night, bendin' bed coils.
                 You a queen, therefore I treat you royal.
                 This is all for you, 'cause I simply adore you.

Chorus:
(Repeat and Fade)

SITTIN' UP IN MY ROOM
from the Original Soundtrack Album WAITING TO EXHALE

Words and Music by
BAYBFACE

Moderately

Lyrics:
Seems like ev-er since the first day we
vest in my hap-pi-

Original key: E♭ minor. This edition has been transposed up one half-step to be more playable.

Copyright © 1995 Sony/ATV Songs LLC, ECAF Music and Fox Film Corporation
All Rights on behalf of Sony/ATV Songs LLC and ECAF Music Administered by
Sony/ATV Music Publishing, 8 Music Square West, Nashville, TN 37203
International Copyright Secured   All Rights Reserved

E7
Em7
met, there is no one else I think of more than
ness. All it takes is just one sim - ple call from
you. Can't seem to for - get, can't get you out my
you. Turn my heart a - round if I'm mak - ing
E7
Em7
head. Guess the ver - dict's in, I'm cra - zy o - ver
ground. Pret - ty ba - by, please tell me if I'm get - ting
Am9
D/E
Am9/E
you. How can one be down? Tell me where to start, 'cause ev - 'ry time you
through. Tell me what is up, you see I need to know. Tell me if I'm

D/E
Am9/E
D/E
smile, I feel trem-ors in my heart. I have but one con - cern; how can I get wit'
far or if I'm get-ting close. I have but one con - cern, my one con-cern is
Am11
Bm11
C/B♭
Cmaj7
Am7/D
G
you? 'Til my day comes, here's what I'm gon' do.
you. 'Til I'm wit' you, here's what I'm gon' do.
Sit-tin' up in my
Em7
Am9
Am9/D
C/D
room, back here think-in' 'bout you. I must con - fess, I'm a mess for
G
Em7
G/A
you. Sit-tin' up in my room, back here think-in' 'bout you. I'm just a

mess with a thang for you. Pray that you'll in - you.

How can one be down? Tell me where to start, 'cause ev - 'ry time you smile, I feel trem - ors in my heart. I have but one con -

cern: How can I get wit' you? 'Til my day comes, here's what I'm gonna do... Sit-tin' up in my room, back here think-in' 'bout you. I must confess, I'm a mess for you. Sit-tin' up in my room, back here think-in' 'bout you. I'm just a mess with a thang for you. Sit-tin' up in my you.

TELL ME IT'S REAL

Words and Music by JOJO HAILEY
and RORY BENNETT

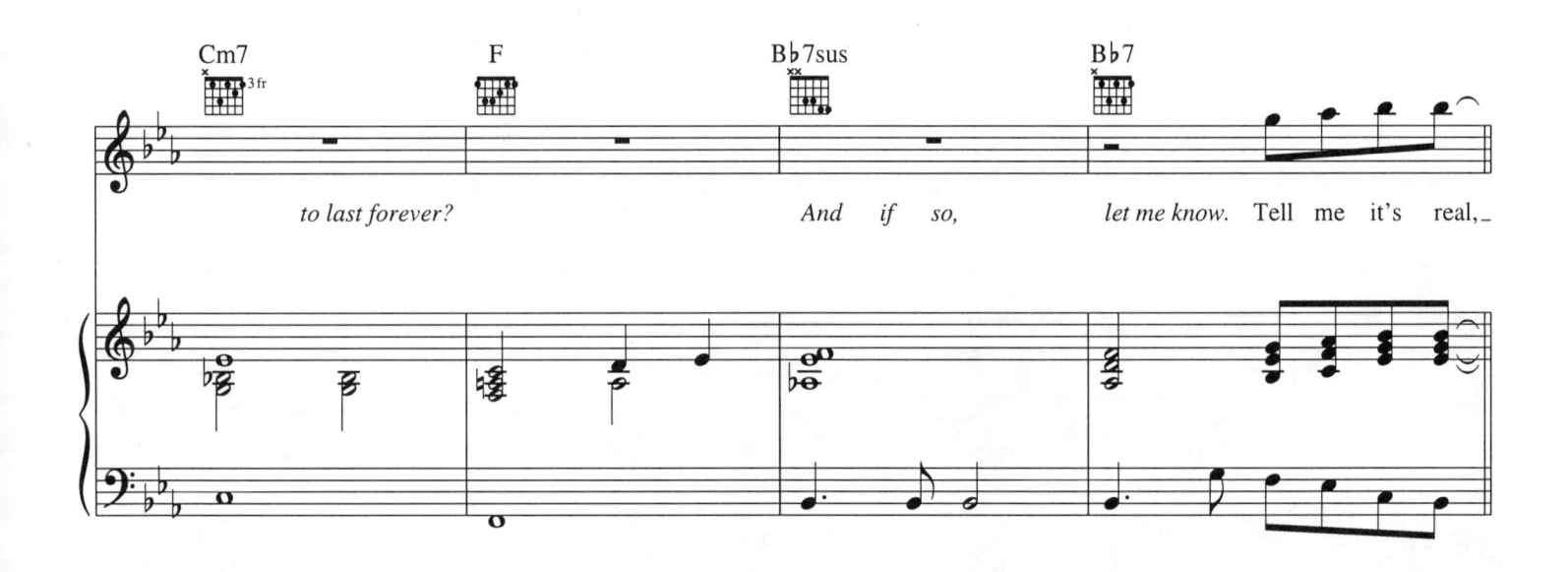

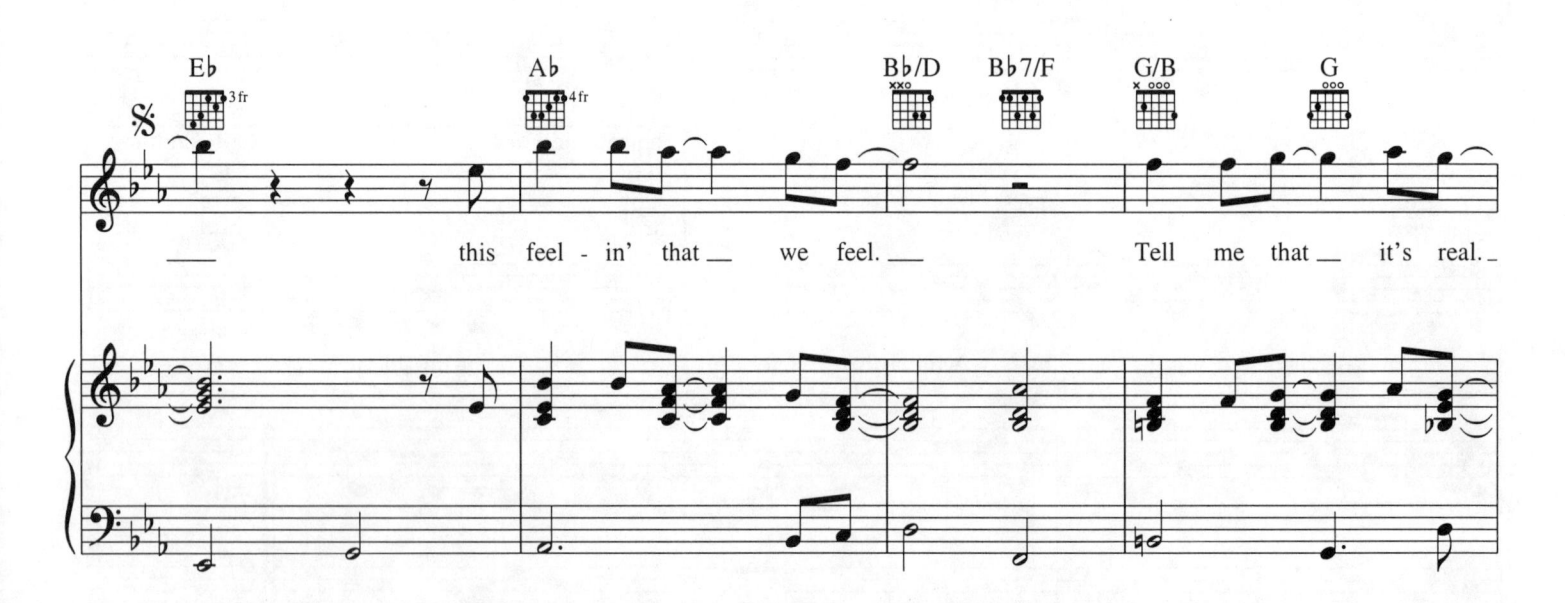

Slowly

(Spoken:) Are you for me like I am for you? Can we share love to last forever? And if so, let me know. Tell me it's real, this feel-in' that we feel. Tell me that it's real.

© 1999 EMI APRIL MUSIC INC., CORD KAYLA MUSIC and HEE BEE DOOINIT MUSIC
All Rights for CORD KAYLA MUSIC Controlled and Administered by EMI APRIL MUSIC INC.
All Rights Reserved International Copyright Secured Used by Permission

Don't let love come just to pass us by. Try is all we have to do. It's up to me and you to make this special love last forevermore.

Ba - by, you told me that you loved me and you'd nev - er leave my side.

Till the bit - ter end, through the thick and thin, you prom - ised me, ba - by, that you was - n't go - in' an -

-y-where. Yes, you did. Ba-by, keep it real. Let me know just how you _____ feel. _____ this feel-in' that ___ we feel. ___ Tell me that ___ it's real. ___ Don't _ let love come just ___ to pass us by. ___

Try is all we have to do. It's up to me and you to make this special love last forevermore. I can't explain the way you make me feel ev'ry time that you told me that you loved me. And you know you did so many times. Just when I thought that love could never be a part of me, that's when you came along and showed me happiness. Baby, you are the best. I think you're dif-'frent from the rest and I really love you. Tell me it's real,

178

G/B
G
Cm7
F7
Tell me that it's real.
Don't let love
care?
You promised that you'd never leave my side.
Bb7sus
Bb7
Eb
Come just to pass us by.
You promised that you'd always be there.
Try is
Ab
Bb/D
Bb7/F
G/B
G
all we have to do.
It's up to me and you
Cm7
F7sus
Bb9sus
to make this special love

B♭7
E♭
A♭
This feel - in' that we feel,
last for - ev - er more. I'll be there for you, ba - by,
B♭/D
B♭7/F
G/B
G
Cm7
tell me that it's real.
if you'll be there for me, sweet - heart. I thought that we were
F7
B♭7sus
B♭7
Don't let love come just to pass us by.
meant to be for e - ter - ni - ty. I thought you loved me, ba - by.
E♭
A♭
B♭/D
B♭7/F
Try is all we have to do. It's
And ma - ma told me take it slow. Boy, you just don't know an - y -

G/B
G
Cm7
F7sus
up to me and you to make this
thing a - bout love. If you and I were meant to be then you would
Bb9sus
Bb7
Eb
spe - cial love last for - ev - er more.
know. It would show by the end of this song.
Ab(add2)
Bb/D
G7
Cm
F7
Bbsus
Bb
Eb(add2)

TOGETHER AGAIN

Words and Music by TERRY LEWIS,
JAMES HARRIS III and JANET JACKSON

Dance beat

There are times when I look a - bove ___ and be - yond;
Al - ways been a true an - gel to ___ me. ___ Now a - bove,

there are times when I feel your love a - round ___ me, ba - by.
I can't wait for you to wrap your wings a - round ___ me, ba - by,

© 1997 EMI APRIL MUSIC INC., FLYTE TYME TUNES INC. and BLACK ICE PUBLISHING
All Rights for FLYTE TYME TUNES INC. Controlled and Administered by EMI APRIL MUSIC INC.
All Rights Reserved   International Copyright Secured   Used by Permission

G13
2 fr
Dm9
G13
2 fr
I'll nev - er for - get my ba - by.
wrap 'em a - round me, ba - by.
C
Em7/B
Gm/B♭
When I feel that I don't be - long, draw my strength from the words when you
Some - times hear you whis - per - in', "No more pain, no wor - ries
A7
Dm9
G13
2 fr
said, "Hey, it's a - bout you, ba - by, look deep - er in - side
will you ev - er see now, ba - by. I'm so hap - py for
Dm9
G13
2 fr
Em9
you, ba - by."
my ba - by."
Dream a - bout us to - geth -

[Sheet music — lyrics:]

-er a-gain. What I want, us to-geth-er a-gain, ba-by. But I know we'll be to-geth-er a-gain, 'cause ev-'ry-where I go, ev-'ry smile I see, I know you are there smil-in' back at me. Danc-in' in moon-light,

Am7 G6 Fmaj7 C/E
I know you are free 'cause I can see your star
Dm9 Fmaj7/G N.C.
shin - in' down on me.
G/A Em7
(To - geth - er a - gain, hoo,
Fmaj7/G Dm9 G/A Em7
) Good times we'll share a - gain, (to - geth - er a - gain, hoo.

Fmaj7/G
Dm9
G/A
Em7
) makes me wan - na dance. (To - geth - er a - gain, hoo,
Fmaj7/G
Dm9
1
G/A
Em7
) Say it loud and proud, (to - geth - er a - gain, hoo.
Fmaj7/G
2
G/A
Em7
3 fr
) all my love's for you. (to - geth - er a - gain.)
B♭sus
E♭
all my love's for you. There are times when I

look a-bove and be-yond; there are times when I feel you smile up-on me, ba-by. I'll nev-er for-get my ba-by. What I'd give just to hold you close. As on earth, in heav-en we will be to-geth-er, ba-by,

Bb13 5 fr
Fm9
Bb13 5 fr
to - geth - er a - gain, my ba - by.
Eb 3 fr
Bb/D
Cm7 3 fr
Bb6
Abmaj7
Eb/G 3 fr
Ev - 'ry - where I go, ev - 'ry smile I see, I know you are there
Fm7
Abmaj7/Bb
Eb 3 fr
Bb/D
Cm7 3 fr
Bb6
smil - in' back at me. Danc - in' in moon - light, I know you are free
Abmaj7
Eb/G 3 fr
Repeat and Fade
Fm9
Abmaj7/Bb
Optional Ending
Fm9
Abmaj7/Bb
Eb 3 fr
'cause I can see your star shin - in' down on me. shin - in' down on me.

UNPRETTY

Words and Music by DALLAS AUSTIN
and TIONNE WATKINS

Medium steady beat

I wish I could tie you up__ in my__ shoes,__ make you feel un-pret-ty, too.
Nev-er in-se-cure un-til__ I met__ you.__ Now I'm be-in' stu-pid.

*Vocal line is written an octave higher than sung.

© 1999 EMI BLACKWOOD MUSIC INC., CYPTRON MUSIC, EMI APRIL MUSIC INC. and GRUNGE GIRL MUSIC
All Rights for CYPTRON MUSIC Controlled and Administered by EMI BLACKWOOD MUSIC INC.
All Rights for GRUNGE GIRL MUSIC Controlled and Administered by EMI APRIL MUSIC INC.
All Rights Reserved   International Copyright Secured   Used by Permission

*Vocal line is written as sung.

F/A G C G/B C/G F F/A G
cause of you. I try dif - f'rent ways but it's all the same. At the
C G/D C/B F/A G
end of the day I have my - self to blame. I'm just trip - pin'.
I have my - self to blame. Be - lieve I'm trip - pin'.
C G/B C/G F F/A G
You can buy your hair if it won't grow. You can fix your nose if he says so.
C G/D C/B F/A G
You can buy all the make - up that man can make. But if

C G/B C/G F F/A G
you can't look in - side you, find out who am I, too.
C G/D C/B
1
F/A G C G/B C/G
Be in the po - si - tion to make me feel so damn un - pret - ty.
F F/A G C G/D C/B F/A G
Yeah, I make you feel un - pret - ty, too.
2
F/A G C G/B C/G
feel so damn un - pret - ty. You can buy your hair if it won't grow.

F F/A G C G/D C/B
You can fix your nose if he says so. You can buy all the make - up the
F/A G C G/B C/G F F/A G
man can make. But if you can't look in - side you, find out who am I, too.
C G/D C/B F/A
To Coda
G C G/B C/G
Be in the po - si - tion to make me feel so damn un - pret - ty.
F F/A G C G/D C/B
I make you feel un - pret - ty, too.

F/A G C G/B C/G
I make you feel un - pret - ty.
F F/A G C G/D C/B
F/A G C G/B C/G F F/A G
Oh. Oh, oh.
C G/D C/B F/A G C G/B C/G F F/A G
Oh. Oh, oh. Oh. Oh, oh.

Oh. ____ Oh, oh. ____

You can buy your hair if it won't grow. ____

You can buy all the make-up that man can __ make. __ But if you can't look in-side you. ____

Be in the po-si-tion to make __ me feel so. ____

WHEN YOU BELIEVE
(From The Prince of Egypt)

Words and Music Composed by STEPHEN SCHWARTZ
with Additional Music by BABYFACE

Slowly

Man-y nights we've prayed, with no proof an-y-one could hear. In our hearts a hope-ful song we bare-ly un-der-stood. Now we are not a-fraid, al-though we know there's much to fear.

Copyright © 1997, 1998 SKG Songs (ASCAP) and Songs Of SKG (BMI)
Worldwide Rights for SKG Songs Administered by Cherry Lane Music Publishing Company, Inc.
Worldwide Rights for Songs Of SKG Administered by Cherry River Music Co.
International Copyright Secured All Rights Reserved

We were mov-ing moun-tains long be-fore we knew we could.

There can be mir-a-cles, when you be-lieve. Though hope is frail, it's hard to kill. Who knows what mir-a-cles you can a-chieve?

When you be-lieve, some-how you will. You will when you be-lieve.

In this time of fear, when prayer so of-ten proves in vain, hope seems like the sum-mer birds, too swift-ly flown a-way. Yet now I'm stand-ing here, my heart so full I can't ex-plain, seek-ing faith and speak-ing words I nev-er thought I'd say: ─ There can be mir - a - cles, ─

when you be - lieve. ─ Though hope is frail, it's hard to kill.
(When you be - lieve.)

Who knows what mir - a - cles ─ you ─ can a - chieve? ─
(You can a -

When you be - lieve, ─ some - how ─ you will. ─
chieve?)

You will when you believe.

They don't always happen when you ask.

And it's easy to give in to your fear.

But when you're blinded by your pain, can't see

your way clear through_ the rain, a small_ but still re - sil - ient voice___ says help is ver - y near. There can be mir - a - cles, when you be - lieve. Though hope is frail, it's hard to kill. Who knows what mir - a - cles you can a - chieve? When you be - lieve, some - how you will, now you will. You will when you be - lieve.

You will when you, you will when you be-lieve, just be-lieve, just be-lieve. You will when you be - lieve.

You Make Me Wanna...

Words and Music by JERMAINE DUPRI, MANUEL SEAL and USHER RAYMOND

R & B Ballad

This is what you do. This is what you do. This is what you do. You make me wan-na leave the one I'm with, start a new re-la-tion-ship with you. This is what you do. Think a-bout a ring and all the

© 1997 EMI APRIL MUSIC INC., SO SO DEF MUSIC, UR-IV MUSIC, BMG SONGS, INC. and SLACK A.D. MUSIC
All Rights for SO SO DEF MUSIC and UR-IV MUSIC Controlled and Administered by EMI APRIL MUSIC INC.
All Rights for SLACK A.D. MUSIC Administered by BMG SONGS, INC.
All Rights Reserved   International Copyright Secured   Used by Permission

things that come a-long with. __ You make me, you make me. You make me wan-na leave the one __ I'm with, start a new re-la-tion-ship with you.

This is what you do. Think a-bout a ring and all the things that come a-long with. __

To Coda ⊕

__ You make me, you make me. {Be-fore an-y-thing be-gan be-tween us, ___ she was
Now what's bad is you're the one that hooked __ us up,

205

| A♭ | G/B | Cm |

like my best friend, the one I used to run and talk
know-ing it should-'ve been you. And what's sad is that I love her, but

| | A♭ |

to when me and my girl was hav-ing prob-lems.
I'm fall-ing for you. What should I do?

| G/B | Cm |

You used to say it'll be o. k., sug-gest lit-tle
Should I tell my ba-by bye-bye? Should I

| A♭ | G/B |

nice things I should do. And when I
do ex-act-ly what I feel in-side? 'Cause I,

Cm
3 fr
go home at night and lay my head down, all I seem to
I don't wan - na go, don't need to stay, but I
1
A♭
4 fr
G
G/B
think a - bout was you and how you make me wan - na
2 A♭
4 fr
G/B
D.S. al Coda
real - ly need to get it to - geth - er. You make me wan - na
CODA
G/B
A♭maj7
B♭
you make me. At this point,

the sit - u - a - tion's out of con - trol.

I nev - er meant to hurt her, but I

got - ta let her go. And if she may not

un - der - stand it while all of this is go - ing on,

Cbmaj7

I tried, I tried to fight it, but the

Abmaj7/Bb   N.C.

feel-ing's just too strong. You make me wan-na, wan-na, wan-na...

You make me wan-na... You make me wan-na...

1.

You make me wan-na...

You make me wan-na, Come a-long with, you make me.

You make me wan-na leave the one I'm with, start a new re-la-

Lead vocal ad lib.

-tion-ship with you. This is what you do. Think a-bout a ring and all the

things that come a-long with. You make me, you make me.

Repeat and Fade

Optional Ending

You make me wan-na

WILD WILD WEST

from the Warner Bros. Film WILD WILD WEST

Words and Music by STEVIE WONDER,
WILL SMITH and MOHANDAS DEWESE

Moderate Rap groove

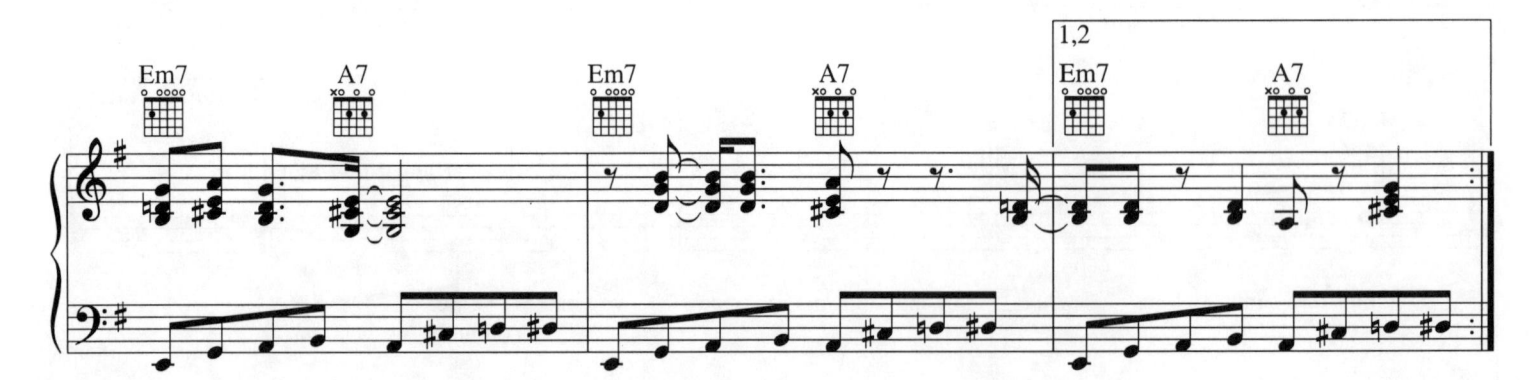

Uh. Wi-ki wa, wa.

Wi-ki, wi-ki wa, wi-ki wa, wi-ki, wi-ki wild, wild. Rap 1 *(See additional lyrics)*

Original key: E♭ minor. This edition has been transposed up one half-step to be more playable.

© 1999 Black Bull Music and Jobete Music Co., Inc. c/o EMI April Music Inc., Treyball Music and Zomba Enterprises Inc.
All Rights Reserved   International Copyright Secured   Used by Permission
- contains elements of "I Wish"

211

212

Rap 2 *(see additional lyrics)*

(Female:) We're go - in' The

213

Do, do, do, do, do. Do, do, do, do, do, do, do.

2nd time only Rap: To any outlaw tryin' to draw, thinkin' you're bad, any draw in the West, that's with a pen and a pad. Don't even think about it. Six gun weighin' a ton. Ten paces and turn just for fun, son. Up to sun-down, rollin' a-round. See where the bad guys ought to be found and make 'em lay down.

Em7
A7
N.C.
They're de-fend-ers of the West, crush-in' all pre-tend-ers in the West. Don't mess with us, 'cause we in the
Em7
A7
Em7
A7
wild, wild West, when I roll _ in-to the wild, wild West, when I stroll _ in-to the
Em7
A7
Em7
A7
(Female:) We're go - in'
wild, wild West, when I bounce _ in-to the wild, wild West. The
Em7
A7
Em7
A7
straight to _ the wild, wild West. _ We're go - in'
wild, wild West, when I roll _ in-to the wild, wild West, when I stroll _ in-to the

1
Em7
A7
Em7
A7
straight, yeah, to the wild, wild West, ah.
wild, wild West, when I bounce in - to the wild, wild West...
2
Em7
A7
G
wild, wild West. We're go - in' straight to the
wild, wild West... The wild, wild West, when I roll in - to the
G/A
N.C.
Em7
N.C.
wild, wild West. We're go - in' straight to the
wild, wild West, when I stroll in - to the wild, wild West, when I bounce in - to the
Optional Ending
Em7
A7
Em7
A7
Em7
wild, wild West, yeah, oh.
Repeat and Fade
wild, wild West... The wild, wild West. The wild, wild West.

Additional Lyrics

Rap 1: West, Jim West, desperado. Rough rider, no you don't want nada.
None of this six-gunnest brother runnin' this.
Buffalo soldier. Look, it's like I told ya.

Any damsel that's in distress be outta that dress when she meet Jim West.
Rough neck, so go check the law and abide.
Watch your step, will flex and get a hole in your side.
Swallow your pride. Don't let your lip react.

You don't wanna see my hand where by hip be at.
Wit' Artemis from the start of this runnin' the game.
James West tamin' the West, so remember the name.

Now, who you gonna call? Not the G.B.'s.
Now, who you gonna call? J. Dub 'n' A.G.
If you have a rift with either one of us,
Break out before you get bumrushed at...

Chorus:

Rap 2: Now, once upon a time in the West,
Madman lost his damn mind in the West.
Loveless, gettin' half a dime, nuttin' less.
Now I must put his behind to the test.
Then through the shadows, in the saddle, ready for battle.
Bring all your boys in, here come the poison.
Behind my back, all that riffin' you did.

Front and center, now where your lip at kid?
Who that is? A mean brother bound for your health.
Lookin' damn good though, if I could say it myself.
Told me Loveless is a madman, but I don't fear that.

He got mad weapons, too? Ain't tryin' to hear that.
Try'n to bring down me, the champion?
When y'all clowns gon' see that it can't be done?
Understand me, son, I'm the slickest there is.
I'm the quickest there is. Did I say I'm the slickest there is?
So, if you barkin' up the wrong tree we comin'.
Don't be startin' nothin'. Me and my partner gonna
Test your chest, Loveless.
Can't stand the heat? Then get out the wild, wild... *(See chorus)*

Chorus:

YOU'RE MAKIN' ME HIGH

Words and Music by BABYFACE
and BRYCE WILSON

Moderately slow funk

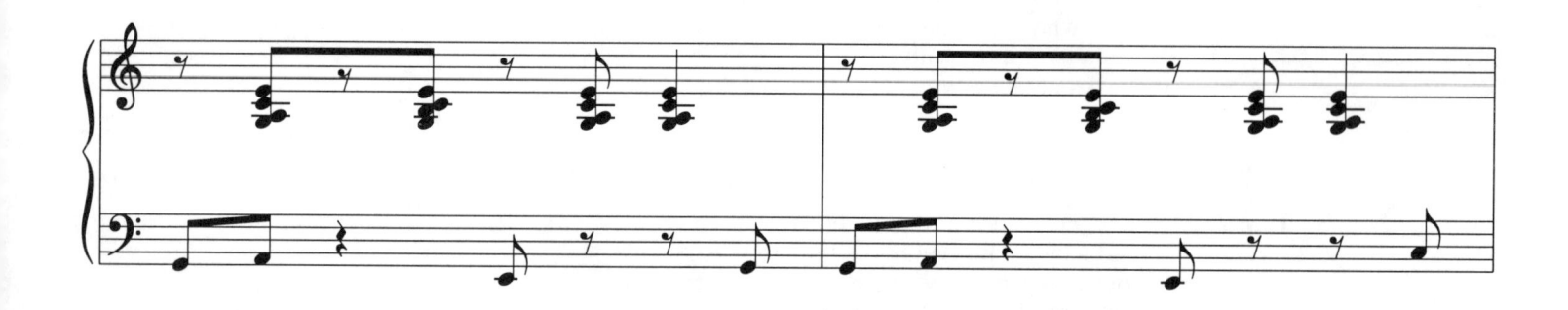

Copyright © 1996 Sony/ATV Songs LLC, ECAF Music, Almo Music Corp. and Groove 78 Music
All Rights on behalf of Sony/ATV Songs LLC and ECAF Music Administered by Sony/ATV Music Publishing, 8 Music Square West, Nashville, TN 37203
International Copyright Secured All Rights Reserved

I'll always think of you inside of my private thoughts.
Can't get my mind off you, I think I might be obsessed.
I can imagine you touching my private parts.
The very thought of you makes me want to get undressed.
And just the thought of you, I can't help but touch myself.
I wanna be with you in spite of what my heart says.
That's why I want you so bad. Just one night of
I guess I want you too bad. All I want is

(1.) moon - light with you there be - side __ me,
(2., D.S.) moon - light with you there in - side __ me, all night,

doin' it a - gain __ and a - gain. _____

You know I want you so bad, _____ ba - by, ba - by, ba - by,

ba - by, ba - by, ba - by, ba - by. Ooh, I get so high

when I'm a-round you, ba-by. I can touch the sky.

Am7/D

You make my tem-per-a-ture rise.

Am7

To Coda ⊕

You're mak-in' me high,

1. ba-by, ba-by, ba-by, ba-by.
2. ba-by, ba-by, ba-by, ba-by.

| Em7 | Dm7 |

I want to feel ___ your heart and soul in-side of me. ___

| Em7 | Dm7 |

Let's make a deal. You roll, I lick, and we can go fly-

| Am7 | G |

-ing in-to ec-sta-sy. Oh, dar-lin', you and me.

| Dm7 | E7+ |

Light my fire, blow my flame, take me, take me, take me a-way. ___

Lord, I real-ly want it, baby, ba - by, ba - by, ba - by.

Ooh, I get so high when I'm a-round you, ba-by. I can touch the sky. You make my tem-pera-ture rise. You're mak-in' me high, ba-by, ba-by, ba-by, ba-by.

Repeat and Fade